Addressing Alleged Bible Contradictions And Exposing Bible Corruptions

The Apologetic Series, Volume 2

Justin Horn

Published by Justin Horn, 2024.

Table of Contents

How I Know The Bible Is Reliable?
(Book Introduction)

Is the bible trustworthy or not? At first glance the title of this book may seem like a paradox, but is it? The primary focus of this book is to show that the bible narrative as a whole (the thousands of underlying Hebrew and Greek manuscripts) are trustworthy, but this does not mean that every translation of those manuscripts are reliable.

The bible is an amazing book. It is the best selling book. It is the most hated book. It was written by forty or more authors over the coarse of over fifteen hundred years. Why should you trust the bible however? After all it does contain hard to believe (for some at least) accounts of talking snakes, a man being swallowed by a whale, Jesus walking on water, people being raised back to life, etc. With such fantastical tales of miraculous proportions, the bible better give us some good reasons to trust it. Well, in my last book I gave 300 such reasons as to why you should trust the bible, believe that God exist, and believe that the earth is young (this book is part 2 in a hopefully three-part series). For the Intro of this book I will be giving you...

Five Reason's You Can Trust Scripture.

1. Available Manuscript Evidence.

The first reason that I would like to give as to why you should trust the bible is because it has more manuscripts that are written more closely to the originals than any other ancient text. Consider the following examples:

Title / # Manuscripts / Originally written / Earliest Copy

Caesar Gallic Wars **251** 100 to 40 B.C 9th Century

Plato Tetralogies **210** 400 B.C 895 A.D

Herodotus History **109** 480 to 425 B.C 10th Century

Greek NT **5,795** 50 to 100 A.D 130 A.D

for a few more examples please see link below.

https://www.toughquestionsanswered.org/2012/12/11/how-do-other-ancient-texts-compare-to-the-new-testament/

2. It's Textual Agreement and Scribes Accuracy.

Another remarkable thing about the bible is that the supporting manuscript evidence lines up with amazing accuracy. According to "The Identity Of The New Testament Text 2" by Wilbur Pickering. "100% of the MSS agree as to, say, 50% of the Text; 99% agree as to another 40%; over 95% agree as to another 4%; over 90% agree as to another 2%; over 80% agree as to another 2%; only for 2% or so of the Text do less than 80% of the MSS agree, and most of those cases occur in Revelation."

https://puritanboard.com/threads/what-is-the-authentic-new-testament-text.15134/

The scribes who wrote the bible were exceeding careful when creating the manuscripts. They were not permitted to write any letter or word from their memory, and they had to read aloud and pronounce the words that they were writing. If there was even one mistake on the sheet, it was condemned. If three errors were found the whole manuscript was denounced. The manuscript was destroyed if one letter touched another or if there was an absent or extra letter.

Diane A. McNeil, Ruth 3,000 Years of Sleeping Prophecy Awakened, Xulon Press, 2005, p. 226-227

3. Bible Prophecy.

In my last book "An Overwhelming Case For Christian Worldview" I list only dozens (out of hundreds of Messianic) prophesies that Jesus has fulfilled. According to the book *"Science Speaks" by Peter Stoner* and Robert Newman the odds of someone fulfilling just 8 prophesies is 1 in 100,000,000,000,000,000, or 1 in 10^{17}. To get an idea of what that would be like imagine Texas being covered in two feet of silver dollars, mark one of them and blindfold someone. Tell them they can go anywhere in Texas but must pick just one silver dollar. This would be the chance of that person getting that one silver dollar on his first try.

Of coarse, someone may claim that the NT writers new the OT prophesies and made of the fact that Jesus fulfilled them. The problem with that is, the apostles had no motivation to do so. They were persecuted and put to death for their belief in Jesus, why would they go through all that if it wasn't true.

4. It's Scientific Accuracy.

I have given many of these examples in my last book, so I wouldn't relist all of them here. However here are a few examples of where the bible was way ahead of it's time in terms of scientific discovery (because of divine revelation).

- Life of the flesh in the blood, Leviticus 17:11.

- Rotation of the Earth, Job 38:12-14.

- Washing under Running Water, Leviticus 15:13.

- Springs in the Sea, Job 38:16.

- Letting the Land Rest one year in seven, Leviticus 25:2-5.

- Waste Management, Deuteronomy 23:13.

- Air Circuits, Ecclesiastes 1:6

5. It Contains _NO_ Contradictions.

There are hundreds, if not thousands of alleged so-called bible contradictions out there, but no genuine ones. A contradiction is when something is said to be A and not A at the same time and/or in the same sense. It is my sincere desire that my book will equip believers with the knowledge and know-how to answer said supposed contradictions. Once you have gone through these 330 plus examples it shouldn't be hard at all to answer most any other supposed bible error, since they'll probably be the same kind of alleged discrepancy.

Chapter 1: Genesis-Deuteronomy

It should come as no surprise to us Christians that unbelievers will not understand the bible, they will say that it has contradictions but it is due to their lack of understanding, and not because what they are saying is true. The bible tells us that the natural man does not receive the things of the Spirit (1 Corinthians 2:14, this makes sense because why would God give wisdom, and understanding to his enemies? Let us begin our study on the many misunderstandings that skeptics have of the scriptures, beginning in Genesis.

1. <u>Gen 1:1</u> In the beginning **God created the heaven and the earth.** <u>Eph 3:9</u> And to make all *men* see what *is* the fellowship of the mystery, which from the beginning of the world hath been hid in **God, who created all things by Jesus Christ:**

This isn't a contradiction since Jesus is God.

2. <u>Gen 1:25</u> And **God made the beast** of the earth after his kind, and cattle after their kind, and every thing that creepeth upon the earth after his kind: and God saw that *it was* good. Gen 1:26 And God said, **Let us make man** in our image, after our likeness: and let them have dominion over the fish of the sea, and over the fowl of the air, and over the cattle, and over all the earth, and over every creeping thing that creepeth upon the earth. <u>Gen 2:19</u> And out of the ground the **LORD God formed every beast** of the field, and every fowl of the air; and **brought *them* unto Adam** to see what he would call them: and whatsoever Adam called every living creature, that *was* the name thereof.

The supposed contradiction is stated as, did God make man or animals first? Animals were made first, Genesis 2 is a retelling and a more detailed account of what happened in Genesis 1. God could've remade an extra set of each kind of animal and then brought them unto Adam, hence no contradiction.

3. <u>Gen 1:27</u> So **God created man in his *own* image**, in the image of God created he him; male and female created he them. <u>Gen 3:22</u> And the LORD God said, **Behold, the man is become as one of us, to know good and evil:**

and now, lest he put forth his hand, and take also of the tree of life, and eat, and live for ever:

Was Adam made in or did he acquire God image? One is dealing with his physical appearance, the other his mind.

4. <u>Gen 1:29</u> And God said, Behold, **I have given you every herb bearing seed**, which *is* upon the face of all the earth, and every tree, in the which *is* the fruit of a tree yielding seed; to you it shall be for meat. <u>Lev 11:3</u> Whatsoever parteth the hoof, and is clovenfooted, *and* cheweth the cud, among the **beasts, that shall ye eat.**

So is man only permitted to eat plants, or some animals? These are different points in time with different rules.

5. <u>Gen 1:31</u> And God saw every thing that he had made, and, behold, *it was* very good. And the evening and the morning were **the sixth day.** <u>Gen 2:4</u> These *are* the generations of the heavens and of the earth when they were created, **in the day that the LORD God made the earth** and the heavens,

How long did it take God to make earth? One or six days? He did it in six literal days. The word day in Chapter two doesn't mean a literal one 24 hr day. The word day can have multiple meanings. Example: back in my day we had to walk 20 miles to school.

6. <u>Gen 2:7</u> And the LORD God formed man *of* the dust of the ground, and breathed into his nostrils the **breath of life**; and man became a living soul. <u>Deu 12:23</u> Only be sure that thou eat not the blood: for the **blood *is* the life**; and thou mayest not eat the life with the flesh.

Does life come from breath or blood? You need both.

7. <u>Gen 2:17</u> But of the tree of the knowledge of good and evil, thou shalt not eat of it: **for in the day that thou eatest thereof thou shalt surely die.** <u>Gen 5:4</u> And the days of Adam after he had begotten Seth were **eight hundred years**: and he begat sons and daughters:

Adam died spiritually that day (as in separation from God). Thus he began to die physically also, though it took 8 centuries. God sacrificed an animal to cloth Adam, (a foreshadowing of Christ death for us).

8. <u>Gen 3:9</u> And the LORD God called unto Adam, and said unto him, **Where art thou?** <u>Joh 21:17</u> He saith unto him the third time, Simon, *son* of Jonas, lovest thou me? Peter was grieved because he said unto him the third time, Lovest thou me? And he said unto him, Lord, **thou knowest all things**; thou knowest that I love thee. Jesus saith unto him, Feed my sheep.

So is God Omniscient? He is. God knew where Adam's physical location was, God was calling out to Adam in respect to his relationship with him. Since Adam was hiding due to his sin.

9. <u>Gen 6:3</u> And the LORD said, My spirit shall not always strive with man, for that he also *is* flesh: yet his days shall be **an hundred and twenty years.** <u>Psa 90:10</u> The days of our years *are* **threescore years and ten**; and if by reason of strength *they be* fourscore years, yet *is* their strength labour and sorrow; for it is soon cut off, and we fly away.

There are two explanations to what may be the answer here, either in the Psalms it is speaking of what generally is the case of man's lifespan, and Genesis gives the maximum or (the more likely) Genesis is speaking how long until God floods the earth.

10. <u>Gen 6:19</u> And of every living thing of all flesh, **two of every *sort*** shalt thou bring into the ark, to keep *them* alive with thee; they shall be male and female. <u>Gen 7:2</u> Of every clean beast thou shalt **take to thee by sevens**, the male and his female: and of beasts that *are* not clean by two, the male and his female.

How many of each kind did Noah bring? The answer: two of the unclean animals and seven of the clean.

11. <u>Gen 7:12</u> And the rain was upon the earth forty days and **forty nights.** <u>Gen 7:24</u> And the waters prevailed upon the earth an **hundred and fifty days.**

These numbers reflect different events, the one being the rain fell, the other was referring to the waters prevailing. After 150 days the waters started to decrease (Gen 8:3).

12. <u>Gen 7:4</u> For yet seven days, and I will cause it to **rain upon the earth forty days and forty nights**; and every living substance that I have made will I destroy from off the face of the earth. <u>Gen 8:2</u> The **fountains also of the deep and the windows of heaven** were stopped, and the rain from heaven was restrained;

Did the water come from heaven only or from the earth as well. The came from both, nowhere in the text says that only the rain caused the great flood.

13. <u>Gen 8:4</u> And the ark rested in the **seventh month, on the seventeenth day of the month**, upon the mountains of Ararat. <u>Gen 8:5</u> And the waters decreased continually until the tenth month: in the **tenth *month*, on the first day** of the month, were the tops of the mountains seen.

When were the mountains uncovered? Genesis 8 refers to the ark resting, it doesn't say the mountains were visible yet. They were probably still submerged. A boat can be stopped by shallow water.

14. <u>Gen 10:5</u> By these were the isles of the Gentiles divided in their lands; **every one after his tongue**, after their families, in their nations. <u>Gen 11:1</u> And the **whole earth was of one language**, and of one speech.

In this instance Genesis 10 is describing events that occurred after Genesis 11. Simple.

15. <u>Gen 16:15</u> And **Hagar bare Abram a son**: and Abram called his son's name, which Hagar bare, Ishmael. <u>Heb 11:17</u> By faith Abraham, when he was tried, offered up Isaac: and he that had received the promises offered up his **only begotten *son,***

Isaac was referring to Abram's only begotten son either because Ismael was sent away or because Isaac was the son of promise.

16.<u>Gen 17:25</u> And Ishmael his son *was* **thirteen years old**, when he was circumcised in the flesh of his foreskin. <u>Gen 21:14</u> And Abraham rose up early in the morning, and took bread, and a bottle of water, and gave *it* unto Hagar, putting *it* on her shoulder, **and the child**, and sent her away: and she departed, and wandered in the wilderness of Beersheba.

There is a possibility that much older cultures aged slower than they do today. Since people lived for hundreds of years in the past it makes since that they matured slower. There is evidence from Paleo-anthropology that this is the case. See, Youtube: The Truth about Ancient Man Dr. Jack Cuozoo

17. <u>Gen 19:1</u> And there came **two angels** to Sodom at even; and Lot sat in the gate of Sodom: and Lot seeing *them* rose up to meet them; and he bowed himself with his face toward the ground; <u>Gen 19:24</u> Then the **LORD rained upon Sodom and upon Gomorrah** brimstone and fire from the LORD out of heaven;

So who destroyed Sodom? Was it God or the angels. Two possibilities, the angels done it and God got the credit since he is God. Or what I believe is that the angels drew Lot and his family out while the Lord burned Sodom.

18.<u>Gen 19:8</u> Behold now, **I have two daughters which have not known man; let me, I pray you, bring them out unto you**, and do ye to them as *is* good in your eyes: only unto these men do nothing; for therefore came they under the shadow of my roof. <u>2Pe 2:7</u> And delivered **just Lot**, vexed with the filthy conversation of the wicked:

Was Lot just or wicked? Lot wasn't perfect in the since that he never sinned, he was positionally righteous because of Christ's sacrifice just as we are. Given the circumstances he did what he thought was best.

19.<u>Gen 20:12</u> And yet indeed *she is* **my sister**; she *is* the daughter of my father, but not the daughter of my mother; and she became my wife. <u>Lev 18:9</u> The nakedness of thy sister, the daughter of thy father, or daughter of thy mother, *whether she be* born at home, or born abroad, *even* **their nakedness thou shalt not uncover.**

Is incest a sin? The law against incest wasn't given until after Abraham, thus it wasn't a sin at Abraham's time. The gene pool was less deteriorated at the beginning so birth defects due to marrying close relatives probably wasn't an issue.

20. <u>Gen 21:31</u> Wherefore he called that place **Beersheba**; because there they sware both of them. <u>Gen 26:33</u> And he called it Shebah: therefore the name of the city *is* **Beersheba** unto this day.

Who named the well Beersheba? Abraham or Isaac? There are multiple possibilities for an answer to this supposed contradiction. 1. There can be two different wells called beersheba, or Isaac could've re-christianed the same well with the title that his father gave earlier.

21. <u>Gen 39:20</u> And Joseph's master took him, and put him into the prison, a place where the king's **prisoners** *were* **bound**: and he was there in the prison. <u>Gen 39:22</u> And the keeper of the prison committed to Joseph's hand all the prisoners that *were* in the prison; and **whatsoever they did there, he was the doer** *of it.*

Was Joseph bound in prison or no? These could be referring to two different points in time.

22. <u>Gen 44:20</u> And we said unto my lord, We have a father, an old man, and a child of his old age, **a little one**; and his brother is dead, and he alone is left of his mother, and his father loveth him. <u>Gen 46:21</u> And the **sons of Benjamin** *were* Belah, and Becher, and Ashbel, Gera, and Naaman, Ehi, and Rosh, Muppim, and Huppim, and Ard.

Was Benjamin a child or adult when he came to Egypt? There are three explanations to this alleged contradiction. 1. Benjamin's brothers could've exaggerated his age when speaking to Joseph in an attempt to persuade Joseph not to require them to bring him. 2. Since Benjamin was the youngest his brother's may call him the "little" brother. 3. Benjamin's sons may have been born in Egypt.

23. <u>Gen 50:13</u> For his sons carried him into the land of Canaan, and buried him in the cave of the field of **Machpelah**, which Abraham bought with the field for a possession of a buryingplace of Ephron the Hittite, before Mamre. Act 7:15 So Jacob went down into Egypt, and died, he, and our fathers, <u>Act 7:16</u> And were carried over into **Sychem**, and laid in the sepulchre that Abraham bought for a sum of money of the sons of Emmor *the father* of Sychem.

Jacob was buried in Machpelah. The fathers (Jacob's sons) were buried in Sychem. The Greek word died in verse 15 is singular "referring to Jacob, but the phrase "carried over" is plural meaning it was referring to Joseph and his brethren. The text does not necessarily say Jacob was buried in Sychem.

24.<u>Exo 1:9</u> And he said unto his people, Behold, the people of the **children of Israel** *are* **more and mightier than we**: <u>Deu 7:7</u> The LORD did not set his love upon you, nor choose you, because ye were more in number than any people; for ye *were* **the fewest of all people**:

The children of Israel started out in small number and then reproduced into a large nation, where is the contradiction?

25.<u>Exo 2:16</u> Now the **priest of Midian had seven daughters**: and they came and drew *water,* and filled the troughs to water their father's flock. <u>Num 12:1</u> And Miriam and Aaron spake against **Moses because of the Ethiopian woman whom he had married**: for he had married an Ethiopian woman.

Did Moses marry a Midianite or Ethiopian? He Married two different women.

26.<u>Exo 3:2</u> And the **angel of the LORD appeared unto him in a flame of fire out of the midst of a bush**: and he looked, and, behold, the bush burned with fire, and the bush *was* not consumed. <u>Exo 3:4</u> And when the LORD saw that he turned aside to see, **God called unto him out of the midst of the bush**, and said, Moses, Moses. And he said, Here *am* I.

Did God or an angel speak to Moses from the bush? The Angel of the Lord is referring to a pre-incarnate Jesus. A Christophany.

27.<u>Exo 3:14</u> And God said unto Moses, **I AM THAT I AM**: and he said, Thus shalt thou say unto the children of Israel, I AM hath sent me unto you. <u>Exo 6:3</u>

And I appeared unto Abraham, unto Isaac, and unto Jacob, by *the name of* God Almighty, but by my name **JEHOVAH** was I not known to them.

What is God's name? He has more than one name/title.

28. <u>Exo 4:11</u> And the LORD said unto him, Who hath made man's mouth? or **who maketh the dumb**, or deaf, or the seeing, or the blind? **have not I the LORD?** <u>Mar 9:17</u> And one of the multitude answered and said, Master, I have brought unto thee my son, which hath a **dumb spirit;**

The Lord or evil spirit causes disabilities? God can use or allow his creations to cause disabilities.

29.<u>Exo 4:21</u> And the LORD said unto Moses, When thou goest to return into Egypt, see that thou do all those wonders before Pharaoh, which I have put in thine hand: but **I will harden his heart**, that he shall not let the people go. <u>Exo 8:32</u> And **Pharaoh hardened his heart** at this time also, neither would he let the people go.

Who hardened Pharaoh's heart? Pharaoh hardened his heart and then the Lord further hardened his heart.

30.<u>Exo 9:6</u> And the LORD did that thing on the morrow, and **all the cattle of Egypt died**: but of the cattle of the children of Israel died not one. <u>Exo 9:19</u> Send therefore now, *and* **gather thy cattle**, and all that thou hast in the field; *for upon* every man and beast which shall be found in the field, and shall not be brought home, the hail shall come down upon them, and they shall die.

Context is key. The plague referred to in verse 6 was touching the cattle in the field, not the ones in stalls, additionally the word "all" could have been referring to the vast majority.

31.<u>Exo 14:16</u> But **lift thou up thy rod, and stretch out thine hand over the sea, and divide it**: and the children of Israel shall go on dry *ground* through the midst of the sea. <u>Neh 9:11</u> And **thou didst divide the sea before them**, so that they went through the midst of the sea on the dry land; and their persecutors thou threwest into the deeps, as a stone into the mighty waters.

Did God or Moses divide the sea? God used Moses, it was God's power.

32.<u>Exo 15:24</u> And the people murmured against Moses, saying, **What shall we drink?** <u>Exo 19:14</u> And Moses went down from the mount unto the people, and sanctified the people; and they **washed their clothes.**

Did the Israelites have water to drink or not? Interestingly there are two occasions between these verses where drinking water is made available to the Israelites after they thirsted.

33.<u>Exo 20:5</u> Thou shalt not bow down thyself to them, nor serve them: for I the LORD thy God *am* a jealous God, **visiting the iniquity of the fathers upon the children unto the third and fourth *generation* of them that hate me;** <u>Eze_18:20</u> The soul that sinneth, it shall die. **The son shall not bear the iniquity of the father,** neither shall the father bear the iniquity of the son: the righteousness of the righteous shall be upon him, and the wickedness of the wicked shall be upon him.

Should children be punished for the sins of their parents? Children will suffer as a result of the wickedness of their parents but we are not to kill others based on the crimes of their parents.

34.<u>Exo 24:11</u> And upon the nobles of the children of Israel he laid not his hand: also **they saw God**, and did eat and drink. <u>Exo 33:20</u> And he said, Thou canst not see my face: for there shall n**o man see me, and live.**

Can God be seen? Short answer is man cannot see God in his full glory and live. Exodus 24:17 gives a description of what Moses and the elders saw.

35.<u>Exo 25:18</u> And thou **shalt make two cherubims *of* gold**, *of* beaten work shalt thou make them, in the two ends of the mercy seat. <u>Exo 20:4</u> **Thou shalt not make unto thee any graven image**, or any likeness *of any thing* that *is* in heaven above, or that *is* in the earth beneath, or that *is* in the water under the earth:

Graven Images ok? Not the one's you worship.

36.<u>Exo 32:14</u> And **the LORD repented** of the evil which he thought to do unto his people. <u>1Sa 15:29</u> And also the **Strength of Israel will not lie nor repent**: for he *is* not a man, that he should repent.

Does God repent? No he doesn't, but from the human perspective he does. Since God is outside of time he already knows what he is going to do.

37. <u>Exo 32:27</u> And he said unto them, Thus saith the LORD God of Israel, Put every man his sword by his side, *and* go in and out from gate to gate throughout the camp, and **slay every man his brother, and every man his companion**, and every man his neighbour. <u>Exo 20:13</u> **Thou shalt not kill.**

Is it wrong to kill? Exodus 20 is referring to the unlawful taking of life aka murder. Capital punishment isn't murder. Under the Old Testament Murderers, adulterers, and idolaters were to be killed.

38.<u>Exo 33:11</u> And the **LORD spake unto Moses face to face**, as a man speaketh unto his friend. And he turned again into the camp: but his servant Joshua, the son of Nun, a young man, departed not out of the tabernacle. <u>Exo 33:20</u> And he said, **Thou canst not see my face**: for there shall no man see me, and live.

Did Moses see Gods face? No, Exodus 33:11 was referring to God appearing to Moses and speaking to in person as opposed to by an angel or dream or something of that nature.

39.<u>Exo 37:1</u> And **Bezaleel made the ark** *of* shittim wood: two cubits and a half *was* the length of it, and a cubit and a half the breadth of it, and a cubit and a half the height of it: <u>Deu 10:1</u> At that time the **LORD said unto me**, Hew thee two tables of stone like unto the first, and come up unto me into the mount, and **make thee an ark of wood.**

Did Moses or Bezaleel make the Ark? Simple, Moses got the credit because he was the leader, even though he didn't personally make it.

40.<u>Lev 4:20</u> And he shall do with the bullock as he did with the bullock for a sin offering, so shall he do with this: and the **priest shall make an atonement**

for them, and it shall be forgiven them. <u>Heb 10:4</u> For *it is* **not possible that the blood of bulls and of goats should take away sins.**

The animal sacrifices under the old testament could not purge one from sins, but were a foreshadowing of the one true sacrifice that could eliminate sin. Animal sacrifices were a temporary covering for sin, they didn't take sin away.

41.<u>Lev 11:22</u> *Even* these of them **ye may eat**; the locust after his kind, and the bald locust after his kind, and the beetle after his kind, and the grasshopper after his kind. <u>Deu 14:19</u> And every creeping thing that flieth *is* unclean unto you: they shall **not be eaten.**

Flying creeping things permissible to eat? It's simple, Deuteronomy didn't list the exceptions.

42.<u>Lev 12:7</u> Who shall offer it before the LORD, and **make an atonement for her**; and she shall be cleansed from the issue of her blood. This *is* the law for her that hath born a male or a female. <u>Psa 127:3</u> Lo, children *are* an heritage of the LORD: *and* the **fruit of the womb *is his* reward.**

Is Childbirth a sin? Or a good thing? Childbirth is a good thing, children are a blessing (Psa 127:3). However Israel had certain ceremonial laws that they had to follow. Similar to how when a man's seed went from him he had to wash in water.

43.<u>Lev 15:24</u> And if any man lie with her at all, and her flowers be upon him, he shall be **unclean seven days**; and all the bed whereon he lieth shall be unclean. <u>Lev 20:18</u> And if a man shall lie with a woman having her sickness, and shall uncover her nakedness; he hath discovered her fountain, and she hath uncovered the fountain of her blood: and **both of them shall be cut off** from among their people.

What was the punishment for sleeping with a women on her period? If it was knowingly they were cut off, otherwise unclean seven days.

44.<u>Lev 20:10</u> And the man that committeth adultery with *another* man's wife, *even he* that committeth adultery with his neighbour's wife, the adulterer and the adulteress shall surely be **put to death.** <u>Joh 8:7</u> So when they continued asking him, he lifted up himself, and said unto them, **He that is without sin among you, let him first cast a stone at her.**

Where adulterers to be stoned or not? One explanation is that since they didn't bring the adulterous man (in keeping with the law), that is why Jesus didn't tell them to stone her. Notice how Jesus didn't contradict the law in his statement. Another thing to consider is the Jews had to abide by Roman law (John 18:31).

45.<u>Lev 21:10</u> And *he that is* the high priest among his brethren, upon whose head the anointing oil was poured, and that is consecrated to put on the garments, shall not uncover his head, **nor rend his clothes**; <u>Mat 26:65</u> Then **the high priest rent his clothes**, saying, He hath spoken blasphemy; what further need have we of witnesses? behold, now ye have heard his blasphemy.

The high priest wouldn't/did rent his garments.

Leviticus is giving a command, Matthew is recording an event where the high priests broke that command.

46.<u>Lev 25:37</u> **Thou shalt not give him thy money upon usury**, nor lend him thy victuals for increase. <u>Luk 19:23</u> **Wherefore then gavest not thou my money into the bank**, that at my coming I might have required mine own with usury?

Usury wrong? Israelites were forbidden to lend upon usury to their brethren (the children of Israel), but they were permitted to lend upon usury to strangers (Deuteronomy 23:20). The New Testament (post Crucifixion) seems to be silent on the issue, though 1 Corinthians 6 may be helpful.

47.<u>Num 5:27</u> And when he hath made her to **drink the water**, then it shall come to pass, *that,* if she be defiled, and have done trespass against her husband, that the water that causeth the curse shall enter into her, *and become* bitter, and her belly shall swell, and her thigh shall rot: and the woman shall be a curse among her people. <u>Deu 22:20</u> But if this thing be true, *and the **tokens of** **virginity*** be not found for the damsel:

How to test a woman's faithfulness? Bitter water or tokens? The tokens were the test on the honeymoon, after that there was the bitter water test.

48.<u>Num 10:29</u> And Moses said unto **Hobab**, the son of Raguel the Midianite, Moses' father in law, We are journeying unto the place of which the LORD said, I will give it you: come thou with us, and we will do thee good: for the LORD hath spoken good concerning Israel. <u>Exo 3:1</u> Now Moses kept the flock of **Jethro** his father in law, the priest of Midian: and he led the flock to the backside of the desert, and came to the mountain of God, *even* to Horeb.

Was Moses' father in law named Hobab or Jethro?

People can have more than one name.

49.<u>Num 12:3</u> (Now the man **Moses *was* very meek**, above all the men which *were* upon the face of the earth.) <u>Num 31:14</u> And **Moses was wroth** with the officers of the host, *with* the captains over thousands, and captains over hundreds, which came from the battle.

Meek people can get righteously angry.

50.<u>Num 15:32</u> And while the children of Israel were in the wilderness, they found a man that **gathered sticks upon the sabbath day**. <u>Mat 12:1</u> At that time Jesus went on the **sabbath day** through the corn; and his disciples were an hungred, and began to **pluck the ears of corn**, and to eat.

Working on the Sabbath OK? There is no specific command in the Old Testament that said you cannot pluck corn on the sabbath

51.<u>Num 16:33</u> They, and all that *appertained* to them, **went down alive into the pit**, and the earth closed upon them: and they perished from among the congregation. <u>Num 16:35</u> And there came out a **fire from the LORD**, and consumed the two hundred and fifty men that offered incense.

These are describing two different companies, the ones that offered incense were burned with fire.

52.<u>Num 20:8</u> Take the rod, and gather thou the assembly together, thou, and Aaron thy brother, and **speak ye unto the rock** before their eyes; and it shall give forth his water, and thou shalt bring forth to them water out of the rock: so thou shalt give the congregation and their beasts drink. <u>Exo 17:6</u> Behold,

I will stand before thee there upon the rock in Horeb; and **thou shalt smite the rock**, and there shall come water out of it, that the people may drink. And Moses did so in the sight of the elders of Israel.

These are two separate instances. The instance in Numbers happened in the desert of Zin.

53.<u>Num 21:8</u> And the LORD said unto Moses, **Make thee a fiery serpent**, and set it upon a pole: and it shall come to pass, that every one that is bitten, when he looketh upon it, shall live. <u>Exo 20:4</u> Thou shalt not **make unto thee any graven image**, or any likeness *of any thing* that *is* in heaven above, or that *is* in the earth beneath, or that *is* in the water under the earth:

Graven Images forbidden or not? It's a sin to worship images, not necessarily making them.

54.<u>Num 25:9</u> And those that died in the plague were **twenty and four thousand.**<u>1Co 10:8</u> Neither let us commit fornication, as some of them committed, and fell in one day **three and twenty thousand.**

Twenty four thousand died altogether, twenty three thousand in one day.

55.<u>Deu 1:15</u> **So I took the chief of your tribes**, wise men, and known, and made them heads over you, captains over thousands, and captains over hundreds, and captains over fifties, and captains over tens, and officers among your tribes. <u>Exo 18:21</u> **Moreover thou shalt provide out of all the people able men**, such as fear God, men of truth, hating covetousness; and place *such* over them, *to be* rulers of thousands, *and* rulers of hundreds, rulers of fifties, and rulers of tens:

Who's idea was it to set rulers over the people? Moses or Jethro? Moses set rulers over the people after Jethro suggested it.

56.<u>Deu 8:2</u> And thou shalt remember all the way which the LORD thy God led thee these forty years in the wilderness, to humble thee, ***and* to prove thee, to know what *was* in thine heart**, whether thou wouldest keep his commandments, or no. <u>Psa 44:21</u> Shall not God search this out? for **he knoweth the secrets of the heart.**

Does God know what's in our hearts. God has intellectual knowledge of all that would happen but only gain experiential knowledge when he witnesses us actually do the thing.

57.<u>Deu 9:10</u> And the LORD delivered unto me two tables of stone **written with the finger of God**; and on them *was written* according to all the words, which the LORD spake with you in the mount out of the midst of the fire in the day of the assembly. <u>Exo 34:28</u> And he was there with the LORD forty days and forty nights; he did neither eat bread, nor drink water. And **he wrote upon the tables the words of the covenant**, the ten commandments.

Who wrote the ten commandments? Moses, or the Lord? There are two possible solutions to this dilemma. 1. Initially God wrote the first one and Moses wrote the second after he broke the first ones. 2. Another explanation is that the "he" in Exodus 34:28 is referring to God, not Moses.

58.<u>Deu 10:6</u> And the children of Israel took their journey from Beeroth of the children of Jaakan to **Mosera**: there Aaron died, and there he was buried; and Eleazar his son ministered in the priest's office in his stead. <u>Num 33:38</u> And Aaron the priest went up into **mount Hor** at the commandment of the LORD, and died there, in the fortieth year after the children of Israel were come out of the land of Egypt, in the first *day* of the fifth month.

Where did Aaron (Moses brother) die? Mount Hor and Mount Sinai are the same place.

59.<u>Deu 15:4</u> **Save when there shall be no poor among you**; for the LORD shall greatly bless thee in the land which the LORD thy God giveth thee *for* an inheritance to possess it: <u>Deu 15:11</u> For **the poor shall never cease out of the land:** therefore I command thee, saying, Thou shalt open thine hand wide unto thy brother, to thy poor, and to thy needy, in thy land.

Will there always be poor or not? Deuteronomy 15:4 is either a hypothetical scenario or referring to the millennial reign of Christ. These are two possible explanations for this apparent contradiction.

60.<u>Deu 16:3</u> Thou shalt eat no leavened bread with it; **seven days shalt thou eat unleavened bread therewith**, *even* the bread of affliction; for thou camest forth out of the land of Egypt in haste: that thou mayest remember the day when thou camest forth out of the land of Egypt all the days of thy life. <u>Deu 16:8</u> **Six days thou shalt eat unleavened bread**: and on the seventh day *shall be* a solemn assembly to the LORD thy God: thou shalt do no work *therein*.

How many days to eat unleavened bread? Six or seven? The former verse included the sabbath.

61.<u>Deu 24:1</u> When a man hath taken a wife, and married her, and it come to pass that she find no favour in his eyes, because he hath found some uncleanness in her: then **let him write her a bill of divorcement**, and give *it* in her hand, and send her out of his house. <u>Mat 5:32</u> But I say unto you, That whosoever shall put away his wife, saving for the cause of fornication, causeth her to commit adultery: and **whosoever shall marry her that is divorced committeth adultery.**

Is divorce permissible? The bible teaches that God hates the putting away (Malachi 2). Jesus said Moses gave Israel the option of divorce for the harness of their hearts (Mark 10). The most lenient scenario is that divorce is permissible in the New Testament in instances of fornication (Mat 5), or possibly if an unbeliever departs (1 Corinthians 7).

62.<u>Deu 27:26</u> **Cursed** *be* **he that confirmeth not** *all* **the words of this law to do them**. And all the people shall say, Amen. <u>Gal 3:10</u> **For as many as are of the works of the law are under the curse**: for it is written, Cursed *is* every one that continueth not in all things which are written in the book of the law to do them.

Those who do the law are blessed or cursed? Answer is nobody kept the law perfectly so they are under the curse but God provided his Son as a way to redeem those under the law.

63.<u>Deu 31:17</u> Then my anger shall be kindled against them in that day, and **I will forsake them**, and I will hide my face from them, and they shall be devoured, and many evils and troubles shall befall them; so that they will say in that day, Are not these evils come upon us, because our God *is* not among us? <u>Gen 17:7</u> And I will establish my covenant between me and thee and thy seed after thee in their generations **for an everlasting covenant**, to be a God unto thee, and to thy seed after thee.

These are two separate Old Testament covenants. One made to Abraham, the other was the Mosaic covenant.

Chapter 2: Joshua-2nd Chronicles

64.<u>Jos 2:4</u> And the woman took the two men, and hid them, and said thus, There came men unto me, but I wist not whence they *were:* Jos 2:5 And it came to pass *about the time* of shutting of the gate, when it was dark, that the men went out: **whither the men went I wot not: pursue after them quickly; for ye shall overtake them.** <u>Exo 20:16</u> **Thou shalt not bear false witness** against thy neighbour.

Is lying a sin or not? There are two possible solutions to this apparent contradiction Either lying is always a sin unless you are doing so in order to preserve somebody's life. Example is what Rahab done here and also the example of the Hebrew midwives in Exodus 1; or lying is always a sin no matter what and the examples of Exodus 1 and Joshua 2 are to be taken as descriptive history and not prescriptive instructions. Similar to how lot's incest and Jacob's polygamy isn't condoned in scripture but is nevertheless recorded. To further support this view consider Romans 3:8 and Revelation 21:8.

65.<u>Jos 7:1</u> But the children of Israel committed a trespass in the accursed thing: **for Achan, the son of Carmi**, the son of Zabdi, the son of Zerah, of the tribe of Judah, took of the accursed thing: and the anger of the LORD was kindled against the children of Israel. <u>Jos 7:24</u> And Joshua, and all Israel with him, took **Achan the son of Zerah**, and the silver, and the garment, and the wedge of gold, and his sons, and his daughters, and his oxen, and his asses, and his sheep, and his tent, and all that he had: and they brought them unto the valley of Achor.

Was Achan the son of Zerah or Carmi? Carmi, Zerah was Achan's ancestor. Son can be referred to as descendant in Semitic language, for example Matthew 1:1.

66.<u>Jos 7:4</u> So there went up thither of the people about three thousand men: and **they fled before the men of Ai.** <u>Deu 11:25</u> **There shall no man be able to stand before you:** *for* the LORD your God shall lay the fear of you and the dread of you upon all the land that ye shall tread upon, as he hath said unto you.

Were the Israelites unstoppable? The passage of Deuteronomy 11 was a conditional promise, dependent upon obedience.

67.Jos 8:28 And **Joshua burnt Ai, and made it an heap for ever**, *even* a desolation unto this day. Ezr 2:28 **The men of Bethel and Ai**, two hundred twenty and three.

Was Ai destroyed or not? In the Joshua 8 reference, forever may not needed be taken literally it could've meant up to that point in time. Ai could've been rebuilt.

68.Jos 10:40 So Joshua smote all the country of the hills, and of the south, and of the vale, and of the springs, and all their kings: he left none remaining, but **utterly destroyed all that breathed**, as the LORD God of Israel commanded. Jdg 1:28 And it came to pass, when Israel was strong, that they **put the Canaanites to tribute**, and did not utterly drive them out.

Were the Canaanites completely wiped out or not? The passage in Joshua is using exaggerated language that is not to be taken literally. It's the like saying the cowboys annihilated the browns at the Superbowl.

69.Jos 11:19 There was not a city that made peace with the children of Israel, **save the Hivites the inhabitants of Gibeon**: all *other* they took in battle. 2Sa 21:2 And the king called the Gibeonites, and said unto them; (now the Gibeonites *were* not of the children of Israel, but of the remnant of the Amorites; and the children of Israel had sworn unto them: and **Saul sought to slay them** in his zeal to the children of Israel and Judah.)

The Gibeonites were to be spared or eliminated? The Gibeonites were to be spared due to an oath made by Israel but Saul ignored the oath and as a consequence their was wrath from the Lord. See 2 Samuel 21:1.

70.Jos 24:14 Now therefore fear the LORD, and serve him in sincerity and in truth: and **put away the gods which your fathers served** on the other side of the flood, and in Egypt; and serve ye the LORD. Jos 22:2 And said unto them, **Ye have kept all that Moses the servant of the LORD commanded you**, and have obeyed my voice in all that I commanded you:

Were the Israelites faithful to God or not? Those that came from were unfaithful and served pagan gods, but their children which passed over to the promised land we faithful up to that point. This is how I reconcile these two passages. I could be wrong though.

71.Jdg 1:19 And the LORD was with Judah; and he drave out *the inhabitants of* the mountain; but **could not drive out the inhabitants of the valley, because they had chariots of iron.** Jdg 4:16 **But Barak pursued after the chariots**, and after the host, unto Harosheth of the Gentiles: and all the host of Sisera fell upon the edge of the sword; ***and* there was not a man left.**

Is God omnipotent or not? God is omnipotent, is was Judah's faithlessness that prevented his victory.

72.Jdg 4:4 And **Deborah, a prophetess**, the wife of Lapidoth, she **judged Israel** at that time. 1Co 11:3 But I would have you know, that the head of every man is Christ; and **the head of the woman *is* the man**; and the head of Christ *is* God.

Woman leadership good, or bad? Men are supposed to be the head. The fact that Deborah was a judge over Israel at that time speaks volumes of the nations apostasy (Isa 3:12).

73.Jdg 4:21 Then Jael Heber's wife took a nail of the tent, and took an hammer in her hand, and went softly unto him, and smote the nail into his temples, and fastened it into the ground: for **he was fast asleep and weary. So he died.** Jdg 5:27 At her feet he bowed, he fell, he lay down: **at her feet he bowed, he fell: where he bowed, there he fell down dead.**

Was Sisera asleep when he was killed or standing? Judges 5 is a poetic song, not to be taken too literally, see verse 1.

74.Jdg 6:1 And the children of Israel did evil in the sight of the LORD: and the LORD **delivered them into the hand of Midian seven years.** Num 31:7 And they **warred against the Midianites**, as the LORD commanded Moses; and **they slew all the males.**

Were the Midianites completely wiped out or did some survive? Well perhaps some did escape the edge of the sword and did flee at the destruction of their cities, we also know that the female virgins were spared.

75.<u>Jdg 11:39</u> And it came to pass at the end of two months, that she returned unto her father, who **did with her *according* to his vow which he had vowed:** and she knew no man. And it was a custom in Israel, <u>Lev 18:21</u> And **thou shalt not let any of thy seed pass through *the fire*** to Molech, neither shalt thou profane the name of thy God: I *am* the LORD.

Child sacrifice is permitted or a sin? I believe that bible scholars have differing opinions on this, some may claim that Jephthah did kill his daughter but this would be an instance of the bible describing a sinful act and not condoning it, if that be the case though, giving God's omniscience of what would happen, why would he give Jephthah the victory? However wouldn't it also be a sin to make an oath and not keep it (Numbers 30). Another scenario is that Jephthah made his daughter be a perpetual virgin until the day of her death. This seems more plausible as she would have been a living sacrifice (Romans 12:1) and it would then make more sense for her to go up and bewail her virginity.

76.<u>Jdg 20:15</u> And the children of Benjamin were numbered at that time out of the cities **twenty and six thousand men** that drew sword, beside the inhabitants of Gibeah, which were numbered seven hundred chosen men. <u>Jdg 20:46</u> So that all which fell that day of **Benjamin were twenty and five thousand men** that drew the sword; all these *were* men of valour.

How many men of Benjamin did Israel slay? 26,000 or 25,000? Keep reading the chapter and pay close attention to verse 46. They slew 25,000 in one day.

77.<u>1Sa 1:1</u> Now there was a certain man of Ramathaimzophim, of **mount Ephraim**, and his name *was* Elkanah, the son of Jeroham, the son of Elihu, the son of Tohu, the son of Zuph, an Ephrathite: <u>1Ch 6:27</u> Eliab his son, Jeroham his son, Elkanah his son. <u>1Ch 6:28</u> And the sons of Samuel; the firstborn Vashni, and Abiah. <u>1Ch 6:38</u> The son of Izhar, the son of Kohath, the **son of Levi**, the son of Israel.

Elkanah was an Ephriamite, or a Levite? Mount Ephraim is a location hence Elkanah was a Levite from Mount Ephraim.

78.<u>1Sa 7:13</u> So the **Philistines were subdued**, and **they came no more into the coast of Israel**: and the hand of the LORD was against the Philistines all the days of Samuel. <u>1Sa 13:5</u> **And the Philistines gathered themselves together to fight with Israel**, thirty thousand chariots, and six thousand horsemen, and people as the sand which *is* on the sea shore in multitude: and they came up, and pitched in Michmash, eastward from Bethaven.

Did the Philistines come back to Israel? Yes or no? Chapter 7 could be referring to the Philistines not coming back to dwell in Israel or it could just be a strong idiom meaning they didn't come back for awhile or at that time.

79.<u>1Sa 8:2</u> Now the name of his **firstborn was Joel**; and the name of his second, Abiah: *they were* judges in Beersheba. <u>1Ch 6:28</u> And the sons of Samuel; the **firstborn Vashni**, and Abiah.

Short answer: two possibilities this discrepancy is either due to a scribal error or the guy has a nickname. Problem solved.

80.<u>1Sa 13:13</u> And Samuel said to Saul, Thou hast done foolishly: thou hast not kept the commandment of the LORD thy God, which he commanded thee: **for now would the LORD have established thy kingdom upon Israel for ever.** <u>Gen 49:10</u> **The sceptre shall not depart from Judah**, nor a lawgiver from between his feet, until Shiloh come; and unto him *shall* the gathering of the people *be*.

So was Israel's king supposed to be from Benjamin or Judah. If Shiloh is a reference to the Messiah we could just say that David was God's choice from the beginning on who should be king. If Shiloh was meant to be a city in Ephraim as some believe it just meant Judah was to rule until Israel inherited the promised land.

81.<u>1Sa 16:21</u> And **David came to Saul**, and stood before him: and **he loved him greatly**; and he became his armourbearer. <u>1Sa 17:58</u> And Saul said to him, **Whose son *art* thou, *thou* young man?** And David answered, I *am* the son of thy servant Jesse the Bethlehemite.

Did Saul no David before he slew Goliath or not? Saul having a temporary lapse in memory (he was demonized y'know) or wanting to know the name of David's dad in no way creates a contradiction here.

82.<u>1Sa 17:54</u> And **David took the head of the Philistine, and brought it to Jerusalem**; but he put his armour in his tent. <u>2Sa 5:6</u> And the king and his men went to Jerusalem unto the Jebusites, the inhabitants of the land: which spake unto David, saying, **Except thou take away the blind and the lame, thou shalt not come in hither:** thinking, David cannot come in hither.

There is no passage that says that only Jebusites could visit Jerusalem. There is a big difference between a person visiting a city and conquering it. These are two different scenario's. Even if the Jebusites were hostile to David when he killed Goliath he could have still put the head outside the gate.

83.<u>1Sa 21:1</u> Then came David to Nob to Ahimelech the priest: and Ahimelech was afraid at the meeting of David, and said unto him, **Why *art* thou alone, and no man with thee?** <u>Mar 2:26</u> How he went into the house of God in the days of Abiathar the high priest, and did eat the shewbread, which is not lawful to eat but for the priests, **and gave also to them which were with him?**

There are multiple possibilities for a correct answer here, which ever one is the case there is not contradiction. The men that were with David didn't show up until moments later after Ahimelech said that no one was with him. Or David's men got there first and the priest may not knew they were together. Or the Ahimelech was referring to other men. Read the context in 1 Samuel and it says there were men with David.

84.<u>1Sa 21:6</u> **So the priest gave him hallowed *bread:*** for there was no bread there but the shewbread, that was taken from before the LORD, to put hot bread in the day when it was taken away. <u>1Ki 15:5</u> Because David did *that which was* right in the eyes of the LORD, **and turned not aside from any *thing* that he commanded him all the days of his life, save only in the matter of Uriah the Hittite.**

David was obedient to the Lord saving the instance with Bathsheba or did he sin by eating hallowed bread? Perhaps because David was to be king that he was not blamed for eating the shewbread or because he was starving, in which case it is lawful to break the law to preserve life. Mat 12:3-7 may be a helpful verse.

85.<u>1Sa 21:12</u> And David laid up these words in his heart, and was **sore afraid of Achish the king of Gath**. <u>1Sa 29:8</u> And David said unto Achish, But what have I done? and what hast thou found in thy servant so long as I have been with thee unto this day, that I may not go fight against the enemies of my lord the king?

David was afraid of or friends with Achish? Things change over time. He was initially afraid.

86.<u>1Sa 23:6</u> And it came to pass, when **Abiathar the son of Ahimelech** fled to David to Keilah, *that* he came down *with* an ephod in his hand.<u>1Ch 18:16</u> And Zadok the son of Ahitub, and **Abimelech the son of Abiathar**, *were* the priests; and Shavsha was scribe;

Abiathar named his son after his dad. We know there are two different Ahimelech because one was killed by Doeg and the other was alive during David's reign (1Sam 22:16, 2Sam 8:15,17).

87.<u>1Sa 31:4</u> Then said Saul unto his armourbearer, Draw thy sword, and thrust me through therewith; lest these uncircumcised come and thrust me through, and abuse me. But his armourbearer would not; for he was sore afraid. Therefore **Saul took a sword, and fell upon it.** <u>2Sa 1:10</u> **So I stood upon him, and slew him,** because I was sure that he could not live after that he was fallen: and I took the crown that *was* upon his head, and the bracelet that *was* on his arm, and have brought them hither unto my lord.

Did Saul kill himself or was he slain by an Amalekite? The answer is that Saul probably killed himself and the Amalekite lied about killing Saul for a reward he though he'd get from David.

88.<u>2Sa 3:14</u> And David sent messengers to Ishbosheth Saul's son, saying, Deliver *me* my wife Michal, which I espoused to me for an **hundred foreskins** of the Philistines. <u>1Sa 18:27</u> Wherefore David arose and went, he and his men, and slew of the **Philistines two hundred men; and David brought their**

foreskins, and they gave them in full tale to the king, that he might be the king's son in law. And Saul gave him Michal his daughter to wife.

How many foreskins did David acquire for Michal? He was ordered to get 100 but went above and beyond the call of duty.

89.<u>2Sa 5:4</u> David *was* thirty years old when he began to reign, **and he reigned forty years.** <u>2Sa 15:7</u> And **it came to pass after forty years,** that Absalom said unto the king, I pray thee, let me go and pay my vow, which I have vowed unto the LORD, in Hebron.

When Did David's son rebel against him? Forty years? Less than forty years? According to some ancient manuscripts (the Syriac, some Septuagint copies, and the Arabic) it says four years in the passage of second Samuel. The writings of Josephus also states this as well (Antiquities 7:196). I hate to say it but the King James may have got this one wrong.

90.<u>2Sa 6:23</u> Therefore **Michal the daughter of Saul had no child** unto the day of her death. <u>2Sa 21:8</u> But the king took the two sons of Rizpah the daughter of Aiah, whom she bare unto Saul, Armoni and Mephibosheth; **and the five sons of Michal the daughter of Saul**, whom she brought up for Adriel the son of Barzillai the Meholathite:

Michal had no Biological children of her own, but she may have raised her sister's children. This is evident from the phrase "brought up". Some ancient manuscripts list Merab, not Michal in 2 Samuel 21:8. That is a possibility in lite of 1 Samuel 18:19.

91.<u>2Sa 14:27</u> And unto **Absalom there were born three sons**, and one daughter, whose name *was* Tamar: she was a woman of a fair countenance. <u>2Sa 18:18</u> Now Absalom in his lifetime had taken and reared up for himself a pillar, which *is* in the king's dale: **for he said, I have no son to keep my name in remembrance:** and he called the pillar after his own name: and it is called unto this day, Absalom's place.

Perhaps his sons died at a young age.

92.<u>2Sa 17:25</u> And Absalom made Amasa captain of the host instead of Joab: **which Amasa *was* a man's son, whose name *was* Ithra an Israelite,** that went in to Abigail the daughter of Nahash, sister to Zeruiah Joab's mother. <u>1Ch 2:17</u> And Abigail bare Amasa: and **the father of Amasa *was* Jether the Ishmeelite.**

People can have more than one name.

93.<u>2Sa 24:13</u> So Gad came to David, and told him, and said unto him, Shall **seven years of famine** come unto thee in thy land? or wilt thou flee three months before thine enemies, while they pursue thee? or that there be three days' pestilence in thy land? now advise, and see what answer I shall return to him that sent me. <u>1Ch 21:12</u> Either **three years' famine;** or three months to be destroyed before thy foes, while that the sword of thine enemies overtaketh *thee;* or else three days the sword of the LORD, even the pestilence, in the land, and the angel of the LORD destroying throughout all the coasts of Israel. Now therefore advise thyself what word I shall bring again to him that sent me.

How many years of famine were offered to David for his sin? It's simple the passage in 2 Samuel was including the 3 years of famine that had already occurred because of Saul(2 Samuel 21:1), and of coarse they had to let the land rest a year (Lev 25:3-5).

94.<u>2Sa 24:24</u> And the king said unto Araunah, Nay; but I will surely buy *it* of thee at a price: neither will I offer burnt offerings unto the LORD my God of that which doth cost me nothing. So David bought the threshingfloor and the oxen for **fifty shekels of silver.** <u>1Ch 21:25</u> So David gave to Ornan for the place **six hundred shekels of gold** by weight.

How much money did David give to Araunah/Ornan? The silver for the threshing-floor and oxen, and the gold for the place. As the text says.

95.<u>1Ki 5:11</u> And Solomon gave Hiram **twenty thousand measures of wheat *for* food to his household, and twenty measures of pure oil:** thus gave Solomon to Hiram year by year. <u>2Ch 2:10</u> And, behold, I will give to thy servants, the hewers that cut timber, **twenty thousand measures of beaten wheat, and twenty thousand measures of barley, and twenty thousand baths of wine, and twenty thousand baths of oil.**

There is a simple explanation to this one. The passage in kings is referring to a gift to the household of Hiram. The second passage refers to the servants of Hiram (the hewers of wood).

96.<u>1Ki 7:48</u> And Solomon made all the vessels that *pertained* unto the house of the LORD: the altar of gold, and the **table** of gold, whereupon the shewbread *was,* <u>2Ch 4:19</u> And Solomon made all the vessels that *were for* the house of God, the golden altar also, and the **tables** whereon the shewbread *was set;*

Omitting a detail is not a contradiction. If there were multiple tables for the shewbread then by necessity there was one (plus another).

97.<u>1Ki 7:14</u> He *was* a widow's son of the **tribe of Naphtali**, and his father *was* a man of Tyre, a worker in brass: and he was filled with wisdom, and understanding, and cunning to work all works in brass. And he came to king Solomon, and wrought all his work. <u>2Ch 2:14</u> **The son of a woman of the daughters of Dan**, and his father *was* a man of Tyre, skilful to work in gold, and in silver, in brass, in iron, in stone, and in timber, in purple, in blue, and in fine linen, and in crimson; also to grave any manner of graving, and to find out every device which shall be put to him, with thy cunning men, and with the cunning men of my lord David thy father.

Was Hiram from Naphtali or Dan? Hiram was of the tribe of Naphtali. In the 2 Chronicles passage it infallibly records the words of the king of Tyre who says his mother is of Dan. She could have been from the tribe of Dan or the city of Dan in Naphtali. Hiram's mother may have been previously married to a Naphtilite or she could have been a Naphtilite who lived in the city of Dan.

98.<u>1Ki 8:5</u> And king Solomon, and all the congregation of Israel, that were assembled unto him, *were* with him before the ark, sacrificing sheep and oxen, that **could not be told nor numbered for multitude.** <u>1Ki 8:63</u> And Solomon offered a sacrifice of peace offerings, which he offered unto the LORD, **two and twenty thousand oxen, and an hundred and twenty thousand sheep**. So the king and all the children of Israel dedicated the house of the LORD.

Could the offering be numbered or not? The number given in the latter verse were just for the peace offerings.

99.<u>1Ki 9:4</u> And **if thou wilt walk before me, as David thy father walked, in integrity of heart,** and in uprightness, to do according to all that I have commanded thee, *and* wilt keep my statutes and my judgments: <u>2Sa 24:10</u> And David's heart smote him after that he had numbered the people. And **David said unto the LORD, I have sinned greatly** in that I have done: and now, I beseech thee, O LORD, take away the iniquity of thy servant; for I have done very foolishly.

So was David upright or did he sin? The bible says that all have sinned and fallen short of God's glory, David is no exception, he was not sinless. However David Generally speaking was obedient to the Lord, and positionally righteous before God because Christ would eventually die for his sins.

100.<u>1Ki 15:2</u> Three years reigned he in Jerusalem. And his mother's name *was* **Maachah,** the daughter of Abishalom. <u>2Ch 13:2</u> He reigned three years in Jerusalem. His mother's name also *was* **Michaiah** the daughter of Uriel of Gibeah. And there was war between Abijah and Jeroboam.

This supposed contradiction is based on the erroneous assumption that a person cannot have more than one name.

101.<u>1Ki 15:12</u> And he **took away the sodomites out of the land,** and removed all the idols that his fathers had made. <u>Lev 20:13</u> If a man also lie with mankind, as he lieth with a woman, both of them have committed an abomination: they shall surely **be put to death**; their blood *shall be* upon them.

Were Sodomites to be expelled or executed? God ordered their death (under the Old Testament) given their were multiple witnesses. King Asa could have "took away" the sodomites by execution. If he simply drove them off it would have simply been an instance of a king disobeying the orders of the Torah.

102.<u>1Ki 15:14</u> **But the high places were not removed:** nevertheless Asa's heart was perfect with the LORD all his days. <u>2Ch 14:3</u> **For he took away the altars of the strange *gods,* and the high places,** and brake down the images, and cut down the groves:

Did Asa remove the high places? He took away the altars of the strange gods but not the altars dedicated to the true living God.

103.<u>1Ki 16:23</u> In the **thirty and first year** of Asa king of Judah began **Omri to reign over Israel, twelve years**: six years reigned he in Tirzah. <u>1Ki 16:29</u> And in the **thirty and eighth year of Asa** king of Judah **began Ahab the son of Omri to reign over Israel**: and Ahab the son of Omri reigned over Israel in Samaria twenty and two years.

How long did Omri's reign last? Twelve or seven years? This could be referring to a Co-regency where the father and son reign simultaneously.

104.<u>1Ki 19:19</u> So he departed thence, and found Elisha the son of Shaphat, who *was* plowing *with* twelve yoke *of oxen* before him, and he with the twelfth: and Elijah passed by him, and **cast his mantle upon him.** <u>2Ki 2:13</u> **He took up also the mantle of Elijah that fell from him**, and went back, and stood by the bank of Jordan;

When did Elisha receive the mantle of Elijah? These are two separate occasions so no contradiction?

105.<u>1Ki 21:13</u> And there came in two men, children of Belial, and sat before him: and the men of Belial witnessed against him, *even* against Naboth, in the presence of the people, saying, **Naboth** did blaspheme God and the king. Then they carried him forth out of the city, and **stoned him with stones**, that he died. <u>2Ki 9:26</u> Surely I have seen yesterday the **blood of Naboth, and the blood of his sons**, saith the LORD; and I will requite thee in this plat, saith the LORD. Now therefore take *and* cast him into the plat *of ground,* according to the word of the LORD.

Did Naboth die with his sons or alone? Just because 1 Kings omits a detail this does not constitute a contradiction.

106.<u>1Ki 22:23</u> Now therefore, behold, **the LORD hath put a lying spirit in the mouth of all these thy prophets**, and the LORD hath spoken evil concerning thee. <u>Exo 20:16</u> **Thou shalt not bear false witness** against thy neighbour.

Does God lie? God doesn't lie and he commands mankind to not lie, God will however permit an evil spirit to lie in order to exact justice on a wicked person.

107.<u>2Ki 1:17</u> So he died according to the word of the LORD which Elijah had spoken. And Jehoram reigned in his stead in **the second year of Jehoram** the son of Jehoshaphat king of Judah; because he had no son. <u>2Ki 3:1</u> Now Jehoram the son of Ahab began to reign over Israel in Samaria **the eighteenth year of Jehoshaphat** king of Judah, and reigned twelve years.

When did Jehoram son of Ahab reign? Both statements are correct. Jehoram reigned as a co-regent with his father.

108.<u>2Ki 8:25</u> In the **twelfth year** of Joram the son of Ahab king of Israel did Ahaziah the son of Jehoram king of Judah begin to reign. <u>2Ki 9:29</u> And in the **eleventh year** of Joram the son of Ahab began Ahaziah to reign over Judah.

Why is this a problem? Even in the U.S we elect the president in November and inaugurate them the following year? The Hebrew word here "malak" could mean become king or reign.

109.<u>2Ki 15:33</u> Five and twenty years old was he when he began to reign, and he reigned **sixteen years in Jerusalem**. And his mother's name *was* Jerusha, the daughter of Zadok. <u>2Ki 15:30</u> And Hoshea the son of Elah made a conspiracy against Pekah the son of Remaliah, and smote him, and slew him, and reigned in his stead, in the **twentieth year of Jotham** the son of Uzziah.

How long was Jotham's regin? Jotham reined as king for sixteen years, however Jotham served as a representative for his leprous father for some time (2Chronicles 26:21). Although the passage of 2king 15:30 mention the twentieth year of Jotham it does not say the 20th year of Jotham's reign, this is because Ahaz was king at the time, however because Ahaz was not mentioned yet the biblical author was keeping time from the installment of Jotham as king.

110.<u>2Ki 18:5</u> He trusted in the LORD God of Israel; so that after him was **none like him among all the kings of Judah,** nor *any* that were before him. <u>2Ki 23:25</u> And like unto him was there **no king before him, that turned to**

the LORD with all his heart, and with all his soul, and with all his might, according to all the law of Moses; **neither after him arose there** *any* **like him.**

Best king was Hezekiah or Josiah? Josiah turned to the Lord indicating was had not always followed the Lord previously.

111.<u>2Ki 23:30</u> And his **servants carried him in a chariot dead from Megiddo**, and brought him to Jerusalem, and buried him in his own sepulchre. And the people of the land took Jehoahaz the son of Josiah, and anointed him, and made him king in his father's stead. <u>2Ch 35:24</u> His servants therefore took him out of that chariot, and **put him in the second chariot that he had; and they brought him to Jerusalem, and he died**, and was buried in *one of* the sepulchres of his fathers. And all Judah and Jerusalem mourned for Josiah.

Where did Josiah die? Megiddo or Jerusalem? Neither text says exactly when he died and thus cannot contradict one another. All we know is that he was mortally wounded at Megiddo and died sometime in the chariot.

112.<u>2Ki 25:8</u> And in the **fifth month, on the seventh** *day* **of the month**, which *is* the nineteenth year of king Nebuchadnezzar king of Babylon, came Nebuzaradan, captain of the guard, a servant of the king of Babylon, unto Jerusalem: 2Ki 25:9 And he burnt the house of the LORD, and the king's house, and all the houses of Jerusalem, and every great *man's* house burnt he with fire. <u>Jer 52:12</u> Now in the **fifth month, in the tenth** *day* **of the month**, which *was* the nineteenth year of Nebuchadrezzar king of Babylon, came Nebuzaradan, captain of the guard, *which* served the king of Babylon, into Jerusalem, Jer 52:13 And burned the house of the LORD, and the king's house; and all the houses of Jerusalem, and all the houses of the great *men,* burned he with fire:

When did Nebuzaradan come into Jerusalem? He could have headed out toward Jerusalem on the fifth month and seventh day and took three days to arrive.

113.<u>2Ki 25:17</u> The height of the one pillar *was* eighteen cubits, and the chapiter upon it *was* brass: and the **height of the chapiter three cubits;** and the wreathen work, and pomegranates upon the chapiter round about, all of brass: and like unto these had the second pillar with wreathen work. <u>Jer 52:22</u> And a chapiter of brass *was* upon it; and the **height of one chapiter *was* five cubits**, with network and pomegranates upon the chapiters round about, all *of* brass. The second pillar also and the pomegranates *were* like unto these.

How tall were the chaptiers? Perhaps the 2kings passage was referring only to the three cubits that had the wreathen work and pomegranates. This is known as a subset fallacy.

114.<u>1Ch 1:32</u> Now the sons of Keturah, **Abraham's concubine**: she bare Zimran, and Jokshan, and Medan, and Midian, and Ishbak, and Shuah. And the sons of Jokshan; Sheba, and Dedan. <u>Gen 25:1</u> Then again **Abraham took a wife**, and her name *was* Keturah.

The Hebrew word Ishshah means wife or woman. A concubine is a wife, though a secondary one. She could have been promoted to primary wife after Sarah's departing.

115.<u>1Ch 8:33</u> And **Ner begat Kish**, and Kish begat Saul, and Saul begat Jonathan, and Malchishua, and Abinadab, and Eshbaal. <u>1Sa 9:1</u> Now there was a man of Benjamin, whose name *was* **Kish, the son of Abiel**, the son of Zeror, the son of Bechorath, the son of Aphiah, a Benjamite, a mighty man of power.

Who was Kish's father? Answer: Ner. Father can mean male ancestor, which is what Abiel was to Kish.

116.<u>1Ch 11:11</u> And this *is* the number of the mighty men whom David had; Jashobeam, an Hachmonite, the **chief of the captains**: he lifted up his spear against **three hundred** slain *by him* at one time. <u>2Sa 23:8</u> These *be* the names of the mighty men whom David had: The Tachmonite that sat in the seat, **chief among the captains**; the same *was* Adino the Eznite: *he lift up his spear* against **eight hundred**, whom he slew at one time.

How many men did the Chief of the captains slay? This is a subset fallacy, he slew 300, and 500 more.

117.<u>1Ch 18:4</u> And David took from him a thousand chariots, and **seven thousand horsemen**, and twenty thousand footmen: David also houghed all the chariot *horses,* but reserved of them an hundred chariots. <u>2Sa 8:4</u> And

David took from him a thousand *chariots,* and **seven hundred horsemen,** and twenty thousand footmen: and David houghed all the chariot *horses,* but reserved of them *for* an hundred chariots.

There were 700 ranks of horsemen with ten men per rank.

118.1Ch 19:18 But the Syrians fled before Israel; and David slew of the Syrians **seven thousand *men which fought in* chariots,** and forty thousand footmen, and killed Shophach the captain of the host. 2Sa 10:18 And the Syrians fled before Israel; and David **slew *the men of* seven hundred chariots** of the Syrians, and forty thousand horsemen, and smote Shobach the captain of their host, who died there.

Ten men per chariot.

119.1Ch 21:1 And **Satan** stood up against Israel, and **provoked David** to number Israel. 2Sa 24:1 And again the anger of the **LORD** was kindled against Israel, and he **moved David** against them to say, Go, number Israel and Judah.

God permitted Satan to tempt David. God did not directly tempt David but allowed for it to happen.

120.1Ch 21:5 And Joab gave the sum of the number of the people unto David. And all *they of* Israel were **a thousand thousand and an hundred thousand men** that drew sword: and Judah *was* **four hundred threescore and ten thousand men** that drew sword.2Sa 24:9 And Joab gave up the sum of the number of the people unto the king: and there were in Israel **eight hundred thousand** valiant men that drew the sword; and the men of Judah *were* **five hundred thousand men.**

800,000 is a subset of 110,000. Concerning the men of Judah the author of Chronicles rounded to the nearest hundred thousand.

121.1Ch 22:14 Now, behold, in my trouble I have prepared for the house of the LORD **an hundred thousand talents of gold,** and a thousand thousand talents of silver; and of brass and iron without weight; for it is in abundance: timber also and stone have I prepared; and thou mayest add thereto. 1Ch 29:4

Even **three thousand talents of gold**, of the gold of Ophir, and seven thousand talents of refined silver, to overlay the walls of the houses *withal:*

How much gold did David prepare for the house of the Lord? 100,000 talents of gold in general. 3,000 gold was prepared for the walls, this is my guess.

122.<u>2Ch 3:3</u> Now these *are the things wherein* Solomon was instructed for the building of the house of God. The length by cubits after the first measure *was* **threescore cubits**, and the breadth **twenty cubits.** <u>1Ki 7:2</u> He built also the house of the forest of Lebanon; the length thereof *was* **an hundred cubits**, and the breadth thereof **fifty cubits**, and the height thereof thirty cubits, upon four rows of cedar pillars, with cedar beams upon the pillars.

What was the dimensions of the house of the Lord? The passage in Kings is not referring to the house of the Lord.

123.<u>2Ch 4:5</u> And the thickness of it *was* an handbreadth, and the brim of it like the work of the brim of a cup, with flowers of lilies; *and* it received and held **three thousand baths.** <u>1Ki 7:26</u> And it *was* an hand breadth thick, and the brim thereof was wrought like the brim of a cup, with flowers of lilies: it contained **two thousand baths.**

How many baths could the sea hold? It could hold a maximum of three thousand baths but sometimes they must of only filled it partly full.

124.<u>2Ch 6:6</u> **But I have chosen Jerusalem**, that my name might be there; and have chosen David to be over my people Israel. <u>1Ki 8:16</u> Since the day that I brought forth my people Israel out of Egypt, **I chose no city out of all the tribes of Israel** to build an house, that my name might be therein; but I chose David to be over my people Israel.

The passage in 1Kings meant up to that point.

125.<u>2Ch 8:18</u> And Huram sent him by the hands of his servants ships, and servants that had knowledge of the sea; and they went with the servants of Solomon to Ophir, and took thence **four hundred and fifty talents of gold,** and brought *them* to king Solomon. <u>1Ki 9:28</u> And they came to Ophir, and fetched from thence gold, **four hundred and twenty talents**, and brought *it* to king Solomon.

Thirty talents could've easily been for the hire of the sailors.

126.2Ch 9:25 And Solomon had **four thousand stalls** for horses and chariots, and twelve thousand horsemen; whom he bestowed in the chariot cities, and with the king at Jerusalem. 1Ki 4:26 And Solomon had **forty thousand stalls of horses** for his chariots, and twelve thousand horsemen.

It seems likely that the first passage was where Solomon kept his chariots, and the second passage was referring to where he kept his horses. Ten horses per chariot.

127.2Ch 13:10 **But as for us, the LORD** *is* **our God, and we have not forsaken him**; and the priests, which minister unto the LORD, *are* the sons of Aaron, and the Levites *wait* upon *their* business: 1Ki 15:3 And he walked in all the sins of his father, which he had done before him: and **his heart was not perfect with the LORD** his God, as the heart of David his father.

Was Abijam faithful? No, but he claimed to be. See Proverbs 20:6.

128.2Ch 15:17 But the high places were not taken away out of Israel: **nevertheless the heart of Asa was perfect all his days.** 2Ch 16:10 Then Asa was wroth with the seer, and put him in a prison house; for *he was* in a rage with him because of this *thing*. And **Asa oppressed** *some* **of the people the same time.**

The bible is clear that all have sinned (saving Jesus), so obviously Asa wasn't sinless. So the question should be what does it mean when it says that Asa's heart was perfect all his days? Could it mean up to that point? Is it saying that Asa obeyed God mostly and in general? Those are two possibilities.

129.2Ch 22:2 **Forty and two years old** *was* Ahaziah when he began to reign, and he reigned one year in Jerusalem. His mother's name also *was* Athaliah the daughter of Omri. 2Ki 8:26 **Two and twenty years old** *was* Ahaziah when he began to reign; and he reigned one year in Jerusalem. And his mother's name *was* Athaliah, the daughter of Omri king of Israel.

How old was Ahaziah when he began to reign? Some claim that this is a scribal error. The word "was" is not it the Hebrew so we cannot be sure that the Chronicles passage is referring to Ahaziah age. It could be referring to the length of years of Omri's dynasty since is was 42 years ago he began his reign (1Kings16:23, 2Chronicles 16:13,20:31, 21:20).

130.<u>2Ch 24:20</u> And the Spirit of God came upon **Zechariah the son of Jehoiada** the priest, which stood above the people, and said unto them, Thus saith God, Why transgress ye the commandments of the LORD, that ye cannot prosper? because ye have forsaken the LORD, he hath also forsaken you. <u>Mat 23:35</u> That upon you may come all the righteous blood shed upon the earth, from the blood of righteous Abel unto the blood of **Zacharias son of Barachias**, whom ye slew between the temple and the altar.

People can more than one name, father can mean ancestor, there is more than one Zachariah in scripture.

131.<u>2Ch 36:6</u> Against him came up Nebuchadnezzar king of Babylon, and bound him in fetters, to **carry him to Babylon**. <u>Jer 22:19</u> He shall be buried with the burial of an ass, **drawn and cast forth beyond the gates of Jerusalem.**

Where shall Jehoiakim die? Beyond the gates of Jerusalem or Babylon? Babylon is beyond the gates of Jerusalem.

132.<u>2Ch 36:9</u> Jehoiachin *was* **eight years old** when he began to reign, and he reigned three months and ten days in Jerusalem: and he did *that which was* evil in the sight of the LORD. <u>2Ki 24:8</u> Jehoiachin *was* **eighteen years old** when he began to reign, and he reigned in Jerusalem three months. And his mother's name *was* Nehushta, the daughter of Elnathan of Jerusalem.

Either a scribal error or it took a decade for him to fully become king. David was anointed King of Israel way before he actually began to reign.

Chapter 3: Ezra-Song of Solomon

133.<u>Ezr 2:5</u> The children of Arah, **seven hundred seventy and five.** <u>Neh 7:10</u> The children of Arah, **six hundred fifty and two.**

Numbers were given at two different points in time, or scripture is just stating what Nehemiah found written in a possibly imperfect register.

134.<u>Neh 5:9</u> Also I said, It *is* not good that ye do: **ought ye not to walk in the fear of our God** because of the reproach of the heathen our enemies? <u>1Jn 4:18</u> **There is no fear in love**; but perfect love casteth out fear: because fear hath torment. He that feareth is not made perfect in love.

Should Christian's fear? We shouldn't fear anything but God.

135.<u>Neh 10:32</u> Also we made ordinances for us, to charge ourselves yearly with the **third part of a shekel** for the service of the house of our God; <u>Exo 30:13</u> This they shall give, every one that passeth among them that are numbered, **half a shekel** after the shekel of the sanctuary: (a shekel *is* twenty gerahs:) an half shekel *shall be* the offering of the LORD.

Different points in history. Also one is an ordinance of God, the other of men.

136.<u>Neh 13:1</u> On that day they read in the book of Moses in the audience of the people; and therein was found written, that the Ammonite and the **Moabite should not come into the congregation** of God for ever; <u>Rth 4:10</u> Moreover **Ruth the Moabitess**, the wife of Mahlon, have I purchased to be my wife, to raise up the name of the dead upon his inheritance, that the name of the dead be not cut off from among his brethren, and from the gate of his place: ye *are* witnesses this day.

Can a Moabite enter the congregation? They can after the tenth Generation (see Deut 23:3). According to my research the text means they cannot become a ruling member of the church or state of Israel.

137.Job 1:1 There was a man in the land of Uz, whose name *was* Job; and **that man was perfect and upright**, and one that feared God, and eschewed evil. Rom 3:10 As it is written, **There is none righteous, no, not one:**

The passage in Romans is stating that all have sinned. Perfect doesn't mean sinless.

138.Job 2:7 So went Satan forth from the presence of the LORD, and **smote Job with sore boils from the sole of his foot unto his crown.** Pro 12:21 **There shall no evil happen to the just**: but the wicked shall be filled with mischief.

Proverbs are speaking generally.

139.Job 14:12 So man lieth down, and riseth not: till the heavens *be* no more, **they shall not awake, nor be raised out of their sleep.** Luk 16:23 And **in hell he lift up his eyes, being in torments,** and seeth Abraham afar off, and Lazarus in his bosom.

Job is referring to the body. Luke is referring to the soul or spirit.

140.Job 21:7 **Wherefore do the wicked live, become old**, yea, are mighty in power? Psa 55:23 But thou, O God, shalt bring them down into the pit of destruction: **bloody and deceitful men shall not live out half their days;** but I will trust in thee.

Do the wicked live long yes or no? This is an equivocation and a sweeping generalization fallacy. Long is quite subjective, humans live longer than dogs usually but not as long as tortoises usually. Also in general the lives of the wicked are cut short (Proverbs 10:27) but God may give some wicked people more time to repent before eternally condemning them.

141.Job 38:4 **Where wast thou when I laid the foundations of the earth?** declare, if thou hast understanding. Job 38:5 Who hath laid the measures thereof, if thou knowest? or who hath stretched the line upon it? Job 38:6 Whereupon are the foundations thereof fastened? or who laid the corner stone thereof; Job 38:7 **When the morning stars sang together**, and all the sons of God shouted for joy? Gen 1:15 And let them be for lights in the firmament of the heaven to give light upon the earth: and it was so. Gen 1:16 And God made two great lights; the greater light to rule the day, and the lesser light to rule the night: *he made* **the stars also.** <u>Gen 1:17</u> And God set them in the firmament of the heaven to give light upon the earth, <u>Gen 1:18</u> And to rule over the day and over the night, and to divide the light from the darkness: and God saw that *it was* good. <u>Gen 1:19</u> And the evening and the morning were **the fourth day.**

Were stars absent or present when God laid the foundations of the earth. Two possibilities here. Either the stars in job are referring to angels or we must keep in mind that although the stars were made on day four, the entire creation wasn't finished until day six.

142.<u>Psa 5:5</u> The foolish shall not stand in thy sight: **thou hatest all workers of iniquity.** <u>Joh 3:16</u> **For God so loved the world,** that he gave his only begotten Son, that whosoever believeth in him should not perish, but have everlasting life.

Does God love everyone? My personal conviction on the matter is that God has loved everyone and has given everyone a chance at salvation, but to those who continually refuse to humble themselves and believe the gospel, well...God's love may just have a limit. God's mercy has a time limit, and whether it's in this life or the next we should all take sin seriously. Here are a few passages that may imply that God's love is not infinite to those who rebel. (Hosea 9:15, Mark 3:29, 2 Thessalonians 2:10-12, Hebrews 6:4-8).

143.<u>Psa 14:3</u> They are all gone aside, they are *all* together become filthy: *there is* **none that doeth good**, no, not one. <u>2Co 5:10</u> For we must all appear before the judgment seat of Christ; that every one may receive the things *done* in *his* body, **according to that he hath done, whether *it be* good or bad.**

Can man do good? Yes, if they are in Christ (John 15:4), with the right motives, following the Father's will. But man outside of Christ cannot do good, for he has selfish or impure motives.

144.<u>Psa 30:5</u> For his **anger *endureth but* a moment;** in his favour *is* life: weeping may endure for a night, but joy *cometh* in the morning. <u>Jer 17:4</u> And thou, even thyself, shalt discontinue from thine heritage that I gave thee; and I will cause thee to serve thine enemies in the land which thou knowest not: **for ye have kindled a fire in mine anger, *which* shall burn for ever.**

How long does God's anger last? A short time for the saved but forever for the lost.

145.<u>Psa 44:23</u> Awake, **why sleepest thou, O Lord?** arise, cast *us* not off for ever. <u>Psa 121:4</u> Behold, he that keepeth Israel shall **neither slumber nor sleep.**

Does God sleep? God doesn't sleep, the reader is taking the writer of Psalm 44 too literally. The psalmist may be saying God is sleeping because he is taking "too long" to act in his favor.

146.<u>Psa 89:36</u> His seed **shall endure for ever, and his throne as the sun before me.** <u>Psa 89:44</u> Thou hast made his glory to cease, and **cast his throne down to the ground.**

Will David's throne last forever? Although by an earthy standpoint David's throne seemed to end, but we must remember Christ was of the seed of David and will rule forever.

147.<u>Psa 104:5</u> *Who* laid the **foundations of the earth, *that* it should not be removed for ever.** <u>2Pe 3:10</u> But the day of the Lord will come as a thief in the night; in the which the heavens shall pass away with a great noise, and the elements shall melt with fervent heat, the **earth also and the works that are therein shall be burned up.**

Does the Earth last forever? Yes or No? There are a few possible ways to answer this apparent contradiction. One is that the word forever doesn't necessarily mean a limitless amount of time. A second way to answer this is that if the foundations are referring to the core of the earth (which is already molten lava) then perhaps it wouldn't be necessary for the Lord to have to reshape or remake it, since it's already hot, if you look at the Strong's Greek dictionary of the word "earth" one of the definitions says (not quoting)it is referring to the part of the earth that is inhabited by people and creatures.

148.<u>Psa 118:1</u> O give thanks unto the LORD; for *he is* good: because **his mercy *endureth* for ever.** <u>Rom 12:19</u> Dearly beloved, avenge not yourselves, but *rather* give place unto wrath: for it is written, **Vengeance *is* mine; I will repay,** saith the Lord.

Mercy to the saints, Vengeance to the adversaries.

44

149.<u>Psa 137:9</u> Happy *shall he be,* that taketh and **dasheth thy little ones against the stones.** <u>Col 3:21</u> **Fathers, provoke not your children** *to anger,* lest they be discouraged.

How should children be treated? The bible is not for child abuse. The passage in the Psalms is written from the perspective of men. Men who were carried away as captives of war. It is understandable their feelings against those who may have killed their friends and family and enslaved them. This however in no way is saying God approves of shedding of innocent blood.

150.<u>Psa 139:21</u> **Do not I hate them, O LORD, that hate thee?** and am not I grieved with those that rise up against thee? <u>Luk 6:35</u> **But love ye your enemies,** and do good, and lend, hoping for nothing again; and your reward shall be great, and ye shall be the children of the Highest: for he is kind unto the unthankful and *to* the evil.

Do we hate or love the enemies of God? We are to love those who are enemies of God so long as they don't try and harm us, war is a different matter.

151.<u>Psa 145:9</u> **The LORD** *is* **good to all**: and his tender mercies *are* over all his works. <u>Isa 45:7</u> I form the light, and create darkness: I make peace, **and create evil: I the LORD do all these** *things.*

God brings evil upon the deserving. Evil can mean calamity.

152.<u>Pro 6:17</u> A proud look, a lying tongue, and **hands that shed innocent blood,** <u>1Sa 15:3</u> **Now go and smite Amalek**, and utterly destroy all that they have, and spare them not; but slay both man and woman, infant and suckling, ox and sheep, camel and ass.

Is killing wrong? Killing innocent people is wrong but the Amalekites were wicked sinners.

153.<u>Pro 11:31</u> **Behold, the righteous shall be recompensed in the earth:** much more the wicked and the sinner. <u>2Co 5:10</u> **For we must all appear before the judgment seat of Christ**; that every one may receive the things *done* in *his* body, according to that he hath done, whether *it be* good or bad.

Are people repaid in this life or the next? Both.

154.<u>Pro 16:4</u> **The LORD hath made all** *things* **for himself: yea, even the wicked for the day of evil.** <u>1Ti 2:4</u> **Who will have all men to be saved,** and to come unto the knowledge of the truth.

Does God make some people just to send them to hell? The passage in proverbs is misunderstood. It is not saying that he made them to be wicked.

155.<u>Pro 16:7</u> When a man's ways please the LORD, he maketh even his **enemies to be at peace with him.** <u>2Ti 3:12</u> Yea, and all that will live godly in Christ Jesus **shall suffer persecution.**

The passage in Proverbs is speaking generally.

156.<u>Pro 24:17</u> **Rejoice not when thine enemy falleth,** and let not thine heart be glad when he stumbleth: <u>Psa 58:10</u> **The righteous shall rejoice when he seeth the vengeance:** he shall wash his feet in the blood of the wicked.

We are not to rejoice when our enemies fall in this life but we will be glad when Jesus returns and establishes justice and punishes the wicked near the end of time.

157.<u>Pro 26:4</u> **Answer not a fool according to his folly,** lest thou also be like unto him. <u>Pro 26:5</u> **Answer a fool according to his folly,** lest he be wise in his own conceit.

These are two different senses. The first tells us not to embrace a fool's standards and the second passage tells us to expose his reasoning so he can see his error.

158.<u>Ecc 1:9</u> The thing that hath been, it *is that* which shall be; and that which is done *is* that which shall be done: and *there is* **no new** *thing* **under the sun.** <u>Rev 21:1</u> **And I saw a new heaven and a new earth:** for the first heaven and the first earth were passed away; and there was no more sea.

From a physical and present sense there is nothing new, but in the future sense and in a spiritual sense there are/will be new things.

159.<u>Ecc 7:16</u> Be not **righteous over much**; neither make thyself over wise: why shouldest thou destroy thyself? <u>Ecc 7:17</u> Be not **over much wicked,** neither be thou foolish: why shouldest thou die before thy time?

Too much righteous or wickedness deadly? The first passage is referring to pride which is wickedness, hence no contradiction.

160.<u>Ecc 7:20</u> For *there is* **not a just man upon earth, that doeth good, and sinneth not**. <u>1Jn 3:6</u> **Whosoever abideth in him sinneth not**: whosoever sinneth hath not seen him, neither known him.

I believe the passage in John is referring to habitual sin, believers do not habitually sin.

161.<u>Ecc 7:29</u> Lo, this only have I found, that **God hath made man upright**; but they have sought out many inventions. <u>Psa 51:5</u> Behold, **I was shapen in iniquity**; and in sin did my mother conceive me.

Is mankind born in sin? Did we inherit sin from Adam? There are two possible answers here either Ecclesiastes was referring to the original creation pre-fall, or the Psalmist was referring to the sin of the mother, not the child. I believe children are innocent until they know what wrong is and do it anyway. Luke 18:16, Romans 2:14-15.

162.<u>Ecc 10:19</u> A feast is made for laughter, and wine maketh merry: but **money answereth all** *things*. <u>1Ti 6:10</u> For **the love of money is the root of all evil:** which while some coveted after, they have erred from the faith, and pierced themselves through with many sorrows.

Is money bad? No, but to love money is.

163.<u>Son 6:8</u> There are **threescore queens, and fourscore concubines,** and virgins without number. <u>1Ki 11:3</u> And he had **seven hundred wives,** princesses, and **three hundred concubines**: and his wives turned away his heart.

How many wives did Solomon have? The higher number was probably recorded near the end of Solomon's life in my opinion.

Chapter 4: Isaiah-Malachi

164.<u>Isa 1:15</u> And when ye spread forth your hands, I will hide mine eyes from you: yea, **when ye make many prayers, I will not hear**: your hands are full of blood. <u>Luk 11:10</u> **For every one that asketh receiveth;** and he that seeketh findeth; and to him that knocketh it shall be opened.

Does God hear our prayers? Yes, if we are obedient (John 9:31).

165.<u>Isa 2:4</u> And he shall judge among the nations, and shall rebuke many people: and they shall **beat their swords into plowshares**, and their spears into pruninghooks: nation shall not lift up sword against nation, neither shall they learn war any more. <u>Joe 3:10</u> **Beat your plowshares into swords,** and your pruninghooks into spears: let the weak say, I *am* strong.

Obviously, reporting on two different points in time.

166.<u>Isa 14:21</u> **Prepare slaughter for his children for the iniquity of their fathers;** that they do not rise, nor possess the land, nor fill the face of the world with cities. <u>Deu 24:16</u> **The fathers shall not be put to death for the children,** neither shall the children be put to death for the fathers: every man shall be put to death for his own sin.

Isaiah is referring to the consequences of war, Deuteronomy is the civil or moral law of Israel.

167.<u>Isa 24:23</u> Then the **moon shall be confounded, and the sun ashamed,** when the LORD of hosts shall reign in mount Zion, and in Jerusalem, and before his ancients gloriously. <u>Isa 30:26</u> Moreover **the light of the moon shall be as the light of the sun, and the light of the sun shall be sevenfold,** as the light of seven days, in the day that the LORD bindeth up the breach of his people, and healeth the stroke of their wound.

This could be referring to different points of time.

168.<u>Isa 40:28</u> Hast thou not known? hast thou not heard, *that* the everlasting God, the LORD, the Creator of the ends of the earth, **fainteth not, neither is**

weary? *there is* no searching of his understanding. <u>Jer 15:6</u> Thou hast forsaken me, saith the LORD, thou art gone backward: therefore will I stretch out my hand against thee, and destroy thee; **I am weary with repenting.**

Does God tire? God does not get physically exhausted as we due to him being a Spirit but he will get fed up with wicked people who continually rebel against him and don't change.

169.<u>Isa 43:11</u> I, *even* I, *am* the LORD; and **beside me** *there is* **no saviour.** <u>Luk 2:11</u> For unto you is born this day in the city of David **a Saviour, which is Christ the Lord.**

Is there more than one Saviour? Jesus is God, so no contradiction.

170.<u>Isa 52:1</u> Awake, awake; put on thy strength, O Zion; put on thy beautiful garments, O Jerusalem, the holy city: **for henceforth there shall no more come into thee the uncircumcised and the unclean.**

This is a supposedly flawed bible verse because historically the gentiles have invaded Jerusalem, but what skeptics need to know is that this is a prophecy yet to be fulfilled.

171.<u>Isa 58:6</u> *Is* not this the fast that I have chosen? to loose the bands of wickedness, **to undo the heavy burdens, and to let the oppressed go free, and that ye break every yoke?** <u>Gen 17:13</u> He that is born in thy house, **and he that is bought with thy money**, must needs be circumcised: and my covenant shall be in your flesh for an everlasting covenant.

Is slavery wrong? Isaiah is referring to a slavery of sin? The bible permits voluntary slavery to avoid starving (kinda like how people work for food stamps), also the bible allows slavery as a consequence for stealing from someone and not paying them back (Exodus 22:3). This is like a better version of our prison system.

172.<u>Isa 60:11</u> Therefore thy gates shall be open continually; they shall not be shut day nor night; **that** *men* **may bring unto thee the forces of the Gentiles,** and *that* their kings *may be* brought. <u>Zec 12:9</u> And it shall come to pass in that day, *that* **I will seek to destroy all the nations that come against Jerusalem.**

The passage in Zechariah is referring to nations that war against Jerusalem.

173.Jer 7:22 For **I spake not unto your fathers**, nor commanded them in the day that I brought them out of the land of Egypt, **concerning burnt offerings or sacrifices**: Exo 29:13 And thou shalt take all the fat that covereth the inwards, and the caul *that is* above the liver, and the two kidneys, and the fat that *is* upon them, and **burn** *them* **upon the altar.**

Does God want sacrifices? God prefers obedience over sacrifice, but will accept sacrifices for those who sin in ignorance or who don't commit capital crimes (Psalm 40:6-8, 1 Sam 15:22).

174.Jer 11:3 And say thou unto them, Thus saith the LORD God of Israel; **Cursed** *be* **the man that obeyeth not the words of this covenant**, Gal 3:13 Christ **hath redeemed us from the curse of the law,** being made a curse for us: for it is written, Cursed *is* every one that hangeth on a tree:

Those who disobey the law are cursed or blessed? Cursed but Jesus pays our fine, if we repent and put our faith in him.

175.Jer 12:13 They have sown wheat, but shall reap thorns: **they have put themselves to pain,** *but* **shall not profit**: and they shall be ashamed of your revenues because of the fierce anger of the LORD. Gal 6:7 Be not deceived; God is not mocked: for **whatsoever a man soweth, that shall he also reap.**

Do we reap what we sow or not? We do reap what we sow, however the Lord has every right to send famine on the wicked and destroy their substance (Jeremiah 29:17).

176.Jer 22:3 Thus saith the LORD; Execute ye judgment and righteousness, and deliver the spoiled out of the hand of the oppressor: and do no wrong, **do no violence to the stranger**, the fatherless, nor the widow, neither shed innocent blood in this place. Num 1:51 And when the tabernacle setteth forward, the Levites shall take it down: and when the tabernacle is to be pitched, the Levites shall set it up: and **the stranger that cometh nigh shall be put to death.**

How shall strangers be treated? Protected or killed? The passage in Numbers is referring to those that would approach the holy things of the Lord.

177.Jer 22:30 Thus saith the LORD, Write ye this man childless, a man *that* shall not prosper in his days: for **no man of his seed shall prosper, sitting upon the throne of David,** and ruling any more in Judah. Rev 3:21 To him that overcometh will **I grant to sit with me in my throne, even as I also overcame,** and am set down with my Father in his throne.

Did Jechonias has someone of his seed ruling in Israel? Supposedly Christ right? Wrong it was Jesus' adoptive father Joseph that had the ancestor of Jechonias, at least by my observation in Luke 3 Jesus didn't come from the lions of Jechonias.

178.Jer 31:33 But this *shall be* the covenant that I will make with the house of Israel; After those days, saith the LORD, I will put my law in their inward parts, and **write it in their hearts**; and will be their God, and they shall be my people. Jer 17:9 The **heart *is* deceitful** above all *things,* and desperately wicked: who can know it?

Should we follow our hearts? Yes, If regenerated and in accordance with the word (Psalm 119:11).

179.Jer 36:30 Therefore thus saith the LORD of Jehoiakim king of Judah; **He shall have none to sit upon the throne of David:** and his dead body shall be cast out in the day to the heat, and in the night to the frost. 2Ki 24:6 So Jehoiakim slept with his fathers: **and Jehoiachin his son reigned in his stead.**

Did Jehoiakim have a descendant sit on his throne? Short answer: Jehoiachin's reign was so brief that it didn't count. The phrase "sit upon the throne" meant a more permanent enthronement, Jehoiachin only lasted three months.

180.Jer 51:24 And **I will render unto Babylon and to all the inhabitants of Chaldea all their evil** that they have done in Zion in your sight, saith the LORD. 1Pe 5:13 **The *church that is* at Babylon,** elected together with *you,* saluteth you; and *so doth* Marcus my son.

Did Babylon Fall? According to some bible scholars the word "Babylon" here is a symbolic stand in for Rome. It makes sense since they both persecuted and/or enslaved Israel.

181.<u>Jer 52:31</u> And it came to pass in the seven and thirtieth year of the captivity of Jehoiachin king of Judah, in the twelfth month, in the five and **twentieth day of the month**, *that* Evilmerodach king of Babylon in the *first* year of his reign lifted up the head of Jehoiachin king of Judah, and brought him forth out of prison, <u>2Ki 25:27</u> And it came to pass in the seven and thirtieth year of the captivity of Jehoiachin king of Judah, in the twelfth month, on the **seven and twentieth *day* of the month**, *that* Evilmerodach king of Babylon in the year that he began to reign did lift up the head of Jehoiachin king of Judah out of prison;

When was Jehoiachin released from prison? The 20th day or the 27th day? The command was on the twentieth but it took a while to process the release.

182.<u>Lam 3:44</u> Thou hast covered thyself with a cloud, that **our prayer should not pass through**. <u>Mat 21:22</u> And all things, whatsoever ye shall ask in prayer, believing, **ye shall receive.**

Does God answer prayers? He does to faithful believers, however the context of Lamentations is in regard to the nation of Israel finally being punished for their longstanding rebellion. God had determined to bring his justice on them (Jer 7:16).

183.<u>Eze 18:9</u> Hath walked in my statutes, and hath kept my judgments, to deal truly; he *is* just, **he shall surely live**, saith the Lord GOD. <u>Eze 21:3</u> And say to the land of Israel, Thus saith the LORD; Behold, I *am* against thee, and will draw forth my sword out of his sheath, and **will cut off from thee the righteous and the wicked.**

The righteous are spared or not? Context is important. Chapter 18 speaking generally. Chapter 21 is in reference to war.

184.<u>Eze 20:26</u> And I polluted them in their own gifts, **in that they caused to pass through *the fire* all that openeth the womb**, that I might make them desolate, to the end that they might know that I *am* the LORD. <u>2Ki 21:6</u> And **he made his son pass through the fire**, and observed times, and used enchantments, and dealt with familiar spirits and wizards: he wrought much wickedness in the sight of the LORD, to provoke *him* to anger.

Does God approve of Child Sacrifice? No, the sacrifice of any innocent person against their will to appease God's wrath is forbidden in scripture. Jesus laid down his life willingly for us (John 15). The passage in Ezekiel is referring to God leaving Israel to their own devices since they were killing innocents anyway.

185.<u>Eze 39:10</u> So that they shall take no wood out of the field, neither cut down *any* out of the forests; for they shall burn the weapons with fire: and **they shall spoil those that spoiled them, and rob those that robbed them**, saith the Lord GOD. <u>Exo 20:15</u> **Thou shalt not steal.**

Is stealing permissible? Under most circumstances stealing is a sin. However in war, God may give someone someone else' possessions (Deuteronomy 6:10-11).

186.<u>Eze 46:6</u> And in the day of the new moon *it shall be* **a young bullock** without blemish, and **six lambs**, and a ram: they shall be without blemish. <u>Num 28:11</u> And in the beginnings of your months ye shall offer a burnt offering unto the LORD; **two young bullocks**, and one ram, **seven lambs** of the first year without spot;

How many lambs and bullocks to sacrifice? These are two very different points in time.

187.<u>Dan 7:14</u> And there was given him dominion, and glory, and a kingdom, that all people, nations, and languages, should serve him: **his dominion *is* an everlasting dominion**, which shall not pass away, and his kingdom *that* which shall not be destroyed. <u>1Co 15:24</u> Then *cometh* the end, when **he shall have delivered up the kingdom to God,** even the Father; when he shall have put down all rule and all authority and power.

Does Christ reign forever? The passage in Corinthians does not say that Christ doesn't reign anymore. Since Christ is God, his dominion is everlasting.

188.<u>Hos 1:2</u> The beginning of the word of the LORD by Hosea. And the LORD said to Hosea, Go, **take unto thee a wife of whoredoms** and children of whoredoms: for the land hath committed great whoredom, *departing* from the LORD. <u>Deu 5:18</u> **Neither shalt thou commit adultery.**

God commands or prohibits adultery? God doesn't force Gomer to cheat, he just knew she would, or has in the past.

189.<u>Hos 1:4</u> And the LORD said unto him, Call his name Jezreel; for yet a little *while,* and **I will avenge the blood of Jezreel upon the house of Jehu**, and will cause to cease the kingdom of the house of Israel. <u>2Ki 10:30</u> And the LORD said unto **Jehu, Because thou hast done well in executing *that which is* right in mine eyes,** *and* hast done unto the house of Ahab according to all that *was* in mine heart, thy children of the fourth *generation* shall sit on the throne of Israel.

Did Jehu do right by God? Read the context in the book of 2Kings. He didn't have a perfect heart in fulfilling God's commands. Just read the very next verse.

190.<u>Hos 8:4</u> They have set up kings, but not by me: they have made princes, **and I knew *it* not**: of their silver and their gold have they made them idols, that they may be cut off. <u>Pro 15:3</u> The **eyes of the LORD *are* in every place**, beholding the evil and the good.

Is God omniscient? God is omniscient. The verse in Hosea means that God did not approve of the rulers that they set up. The bible sometimes uses anthropomorphic language for our benefit.

191.<u>Joe 3:17</u> So shall ye know that I *am* the LORD your **God dwelling in Zion**, my holy mountain: then shall Jerusalem be holy, and there shall no strangers pass through her any more. <u>Ecc 5:2</u> Be not rash with thy mouth, and let not thine heart be hasty to utter *any* thing before God: for **God *is* in heaven,** and thou upon earth: therefore let thy words be few.

Where is God? Zion or Heaven. Technically God is omnipresent, that is, everywhere. But Jesus is currently in the 3rd heaven waiting to descend with new Jerusalem and make the New heaven and earth. He will then rule from Zion.

192.<u>Jon 1:17</u> Now the LORD had prepared a **great fish** to swallow up Jonah. And Jonah was in the belly of the fish three days and three nights. <u>Mat 12:40</u> For as Jonas was three days and three nights in **the whale's belly;** so shall the Son of man be three days and three nights in the heart of the earth.

What was Jonah swallowed by? Jonah was swallowed by a great fish, under our modern classification system it is called a whale.

193.<u>Jon 3:4</u> And Jonah began to enter into the city a day's journey, and he cried, and said, Yet forty days, and **Nineveh shall be overthrown.** <u>Jon 3:10</u> And God saw their works, that they turned from their evil way; and God repented of the evil, that he had said that he would do unto them; and **he did** *it* **not.**

Did God lie? Nineveh's destruction was contingent upon whether or not they would repent.

194.<u>Hab 1:13</u> *Thou art* of purer eyes than to behold evil, and canst not look on iniquity: wherefore lookest thou upon them that deal treacherously, *and* holdest thy tongue **when the wicked devoureth** *the man that is* **more righteous than he?** <u>Pro 12:21</u> There shall **no evil happen to the just:** but the wicked shall be filled with mischief.

Proverbs is speaking generally.

195.<u>Hab 2:4</u> Behold, his soul *which* is lifted up is not upright in him: but the **just shall live by his faith.** <u>Eze 18:9</u> Hath **walked in my statutes, and hath kept my judgments,** to deal truly; he *is* just, he shall surely live, saith the Lord GOD.

Are we justified by faith or obedience? Faith which is demonstrated by works. Works are evidence of living faith.

196.<u>Zec 1:1</u> In the eighth month, in the second year of Darius, came the word of the LORD unto **Zechariah, the son of Berechiah, the son of Iddo** the prophet, saying, <u>Ezr 5:1</u> Then the prophets, Haggai the prophet, and **Zechariah the son of Iddo**, prophesied unto the Jews that *were* in Judah and Jerusalem in the name of the God of Israel, *even* unto them.

Son can mean descendant.

197.<u>Zec 9:9</u> Rejoice greatly, O daughter of Zion; shout, O daughter of Jerusalem: behold, thy King cometh unto thee: he *is* just, and having salvation; **lowly, and riding upon an ass,** and upon a colt the foal of an ass. <u>Dan 7:14</u> And **there was given him dominion, and glory, and a kingdom,** that all people, nations, and languages, should serve him: his dominion *is* an everlasting dominion, which shall not pass away, and his kingdom *that* which shall not be destroyed.

Jesus comes humbly or in glory? There is a first and second coming.

198.<u>Zec 10:10</u> **I will bring them again also out of the land of Egypt,** and gather them out of Assyria; and I will bring them into the land of Gilead and Lebanon; and *place* shall not be found for them. <u>Jer 42:17</u> So shall it be with all the men that set their faces to go into Egypt to sojourn there; they shall die by the sword, by the famine, and by the pestilence: and **none of them shall remain or escape from the evil that I will bring upon them.**

Will God destroy all the Israelites that went down to Egypt? Yes or No? There are at least two possible explanations for this seeming contradiction. Number 1: The passage in Jeremiah could be using hyperbole and doesn't mean that every last Israelite would be destroyed that went down to Egypt. Number 2. Zechariah 10 could be a bible prophecy that is yet to be fulfilled and as such there could have been countless Jews that have moved into Egypt in the past few thousand years and that threat may have been only to the Jews at that time.

199.**<u>Zec 11:13</u>** And the LORD said unto me, Cast it unto the potter: a goodly price that I was prised at of them. And I took the thirty *pieces* of silver, and cast them to the potter in the house of the LORD. <u>Mat 27:9</u> Then was fulfilled that which was spoken by **Jeremy the prophet,** saying, And they took the thirty pieces of silver, the price of him that was valued, whom they of the children of Israel did value;

Why does Matthew attribute this prophecy to Jeremiah when it was written by Zechariah? Matthew was not quoting Jeremiah nor Zechariah exclusively, he didn't give an exact quote. Matthew combined part of these different prophecies to drive a point home. It was common during his time to cite the more popular prophet.

200.<u>Mal 4:4</u> Remember ye the law of Moses my servant, which I commanded unto him **in Horeb** for all Israel, *with* the statutes and judgments. <u>Exo 31:18</u> And he gave unto Moses, when he had made an end of communing with him **upon mount Sinai**, two tables of testimony, tables of stone, written with the finger of God.

Was the law giving on Mt. Horeb or Sinai? Same place, next.

201.<u>Mal 4:6</u> And he shall turn the heart of the fathers to the children, and the heart of the children to their fathers, **lest I come and smite the earth with a curse.** <u>Gen 8:21</u> And the LORD smelled a sweet savour; and the LORD said in his heart, I **will not again curse the ground any more for man's sake**; for the imagination of man's heart *is* evil from his youth; neither will I again smite any more every thing living, as I have done.

Will God curse the earth again? God wouldn't curse the earth with a global flood, there are other types of curses, obviously.

Chapter 5: The Gospels

202.<u>Mat 1:17</u> So all the generations from Abraham to David *are* **fourteen generations**; and from David until the carrying away into Babylon *are* fourteen generations; and from the carrying away into Babylon unto Christ *are* fourteen generations. <u>1Ch 3:10-16</u> And Solomon's son *was* Rehoboam, Abia his son, Asa his son, Jehoshaphat his son, Joram his son, Ahaziah his son, Joash his son, Amaziah his son, Azariah his son, Jotham his son, Ahaz his son, Hezekiah his son, Manasseh his son, Amon his son, Josiah his son. And the sons of Josiah *were,* the firstborn Johanan, the second Jehoiakim, the third Zedekiah, the fourth Shallum. And the sons of Jehoiakim: Jeconiah his son, Zedekiah his son.

How many generations until the carrying away to Babylon? Fourteen or more? Matthew left out some names.

203.<u>Mat 1:20</u> But while he thought on these things, behold, the angel of the Lord appeared unto him in a dream, saying, Joseph, thou son of David, fear not to take unto thee Mary thy wife: for that which is conceived in her is of the Holy Ghost. <u>Luk 1:30</u> And the angel said unto her, Fear not, Mary: for thou hast found favour with God. <u>Luk 1:31</u> And, behold, thou shalt conceive in thy womb, and bring forth a son, and shalt call his name JESUS.

Did the Annunciation occur to Mary pre-conception or to Joseph post-conception? These are two separate events, both are true.

204.<u>Mat 2:1</u> Now when Jesus was born in **Bethlehem** of Judaea in the days of Herod the king, behold, there came wise men from the east to Jerusalem, <u>Luk 2:4</u> And Joseph also went up from Galilee, out of the city of **Nazareth**, into Judaea, unto the city of David, which is called Bethlehem; (because he was of the house and lineage of David:)

Where was Jesus born? Bethlehem, Joseph and Mary traveled from Nazareth to Bethlehem for taxation.

205.<u>Mat 4:5</u> Then the devil taketh him up into the holy city, and setteth him on a **pinnacle of the temple**, <u>Luk 4:5</u> And the devil, taking him up into **an**

high mountain, shewed unto him all the kingdoms of the world in a moment of time.

Did the devil take Jesus to the temple or mountain first? Doesn't matter one gospel just didn't list the events in chronological order.

206.<u>Mat 5:1</u> And seeing the multitudes, he went **up into a mountain**: and when he was set, his disciples came unto him: <u>Luk 6:17</u> And he came down with them, and **stood in the plain**, and the company of his disciples, and a great multitude of people out of all Judaea and Jerusalem, and from the sea coast of Tyre and Sidon, which came to hear him, and to be healed of their diseases;

When giving his famous sermon did Jesus go up a mountain or stand in a plain? Did it occur to the reader that Jesus could have moved around during his sermon?

207.<u>Mat 5:39</u> But I say unto you, That ye resist not evil: but **whosoever shall smite thee on thy right cheek, turn to him the other also.** <u>Luk 22:36</u> Then said he unto them, But now, he that hath a purse, let him take *it,* and likewise *his* scrip: and **he that hath no sword, let him sell his garment, and buy one.**

Self defense OK? Yes, it is. The passage in Matthew is referring to insults.

208.<u>Mat 5:22</u> But I say unto you, **That whosoever is angry with his brother** without a cause shall be in danger of the judgment: and whosoever shall say to his brother, Raca, shall be in danger of the council: but whosoever shall say, Thou fool, shall be in danger of hell fire. <u>Mar 3:5</u> And **when he had looked round about on them with anger**, being grieved for the hardness of their hearts, he saith unto the man, Stretch forth thine hand. And he stretched *it* out: and his hand was restored whole as the other.

Anger a sin? No (Eph 4:26),Jesus had just cause to be angry, therefore didn't sin.

209.<u>Mat 5:22</u> But I say unto you, That whosoever is angry with his brother without a cause shall be in danger of the judgment: and whosoever shall say to his brother, Raca, shall be in danger of the council: **but whosoever shall say, Thou fool, shall be in danger of hell fire.** <u>Luk 11:40</u> *Ye fools,* did not he that made that which is without make that which is within also?

Two possible explanations on calling someone a fool. Either is a sin to call a brother (fellow christian a fool); because of false witness, or Jesus was permitted to do so because only he knew what was in men's hearts.

210.<u>Mat 6:5</u> And when thou prayest, **thou shalt not be as the hypocrites** *are:* for they love to **pray standing in the synagogues and in the corners of the streets,** that they may be seen of men. Verily I say unto you, They have their reward. <u>1Ti 2:8</u> I will therefore that **men pray every where,** lifting up holy hands, without wrath and doubting.

A sin to pray in the open? It depends. Are you doing it to look good in front of others? If so, then it is wrong.

211.<u>Mat 6:9</u> **After this manner therefore pray ye:** Our Father which art in heaven, Hallowed be thy name. <u>Mat 6:10</u> Thy kingdom come. Thy will be done in earth, as *it is* in heaven. <u>Mat 6:11</u> Give us this day our daily bread. <u>Mat 6:12</u> And forgive us our debts, as we forgive our debtors. <u>Mat 6:13</u> And lead us not into temptation, but deliver us from evil: For thine is the kingdom, and the power, and the glory, for ever. Amen. <u>Rom 8:26</u> Likewise the Spirit also helpeth our infirmities: **for we know not what we should pray for as we ought**: but the Spirit itself maketh intercession for us with groanings which cannot be uttered.

Did the disciples know how to pray? Yes, in general. However they may not have known what specifically to pray for.

212.<u>Mat 7:21</u> **Not every one that saith unto me, Lord, Lord, shall enter into the kingdom of heaven;** but he that doeth the will of my Father which is in heaven. <u>Act 2:21</u> And it shall come to pass, *that* **whosoever shall call on the name of the Lord shall be saved.**

Is calling Jesus Lord a ticket to heaven? If you mean it then yes. Matthew 7:23 shows why the others were denied access, because of their iniquity. If you call Jesus Lord, you do what he says (Luke 6:46).

213.<u>Mat 10:5</u> These twelve Jesus sent forth, and commanded them, saying, **Go not into the way of the Gentiles, and into** *any* **city of the Samaritans enter ye not:** <u>Mat 10:6</u> But go rather to the lost sheep of the house of Israel. <u>Mar</u>

<u>16:15</u> And he said unto them, Go ye into all the world, and **preach the gospel to every creature**.

Were the disciples told to preach to other nations or just to Israel? Before the crucifixion Jesus was more concerned with Israel, but after he was raised he commanded his followers to preach to the world (Acts 13:46).

214.<u>Mat 10:23</u> But when they persecute you in this city, flee ye into another: for verily I say unto you, **Ye shall not have gone over the cities of Israel, till the Son of man be come.** <u>Mat 24:14</u> And this gospel of the kingdom shall be **preached in all the world for a witness unto all nations; and then shall the end come.**

Was the end to come during the lives of the apostles or was it to happen much later? The passage of Matthew 10 has been misinterpreted to mean that the end of the world was to happen during the lives of the apostles. The phrase "Son of man be come" was referring to a near-term arrival of Christ, not his last coming.

215.<u>Mat 11:13</u> For all the prophets and the law prophesied until John. Mat 11:14 And if ye will receive *it,* **this is Elias, which was for to come.** <u>Joh 1:21</u> And they asked him, What then? Art thou Elias? And he saith, **I am not.** Art thou that prophet? And he answered, No.

Was John the baptist a reincarnated Elias? Short answer is that John came in the Spirit and power of Elias.

216.<u>Mat 11:30</u> For **my yoke *is* easy, and my burden is light**. <u>2Ti 3:12</u> Yea, and all that will **live godly in Christ Jesus shall suffer persecution.**

Is following Christ hard or easy? Compared to what? Following Christ is easier than living in sin (Proverb 15:19, Eccl 2:26). Sin destroys and makes your miserable, in Christ there is joy, love, peace, and strength.

217.<u>Mat 16:17</u> And Jesus answered and said unto him, **Blessed art thou, Simon Barjona**: for flesh and blood hath not revealed *it* unto thee, but my Father which is in heaven. <u>Mat 16:23</u> **But he turned, and said unto Peter, Get thee behind me, Satan:** thou art an offence unto me: for thou savourest not the things that be of God, but those that be of men.

Jesus commended or rebuked Peter? He did both. Commended him on his belief in who Jesus was but rebuked him for trying to thwart God's plan.

218.<u>Mat 20:30</u> And, behold, **two blind men** sitting by the way side, when they heard that Jesus passed by, cried out, saying, Have mercy on us, O Lord, *thou* Son of David. <u>Luk 18:35</u> And it came to pass, that as he was come nigh unto Jericho, **a certain blind** man sat by the way side begging:

Was there one or two blind men? Just because Luke doesn't mention both blind man, this does not constitute a contradiction. Only if this was the same instance and Luke wrote there was only one blind man would this be a contradiction.

219.<u>Mat 21:12</u> And Jesus went into the temple of God, and cast out all them that sold and bought in the temple, and **overthrew the tables** of the moneychangers, and the seats of them that sold doves, <u>Joh 2:15</u> And when he had made a scourge of small cords, he drove them all out of the temple, and the sheep, and the oxen; and poured out the changers' money, **and overthrew the tables;**

Did Jesus overturn the tables near the beginning of his ministry or near the end? This actually happened at two different time.

220.<u>Mat 24:32</u> Now learn a parable of the fig tree; When **his** branch is yet tender, and putteth forth leaves, ye know that summer *is* nigh: <u>Mar 13:28</u> Now learn a parable of the fig tree; When **her** branch is yet tender, and putteth forth leaves, ye know that summer is near:

The fig tree male or female? It's symbolic, doesn't matter.

221.<u>Mat 26:48</u> Now he that betrayed him gave them a sign, saying, **Whomsoever I shall kiss**, that same is he: hold him fast. Joh 18:4 Jesus therefore, knowing all things that should come upon him, went forth, and said unto them, Whom seek ye? <u>Joh 18:5</u> They answered him, Jesus of Nazareth. **Jesus saith unto them, I am** *he*. And Judas also, which betrayed him, stood with them.

Did Judas kiss Jesus or not? John simply omitted that part.

222.<u>Mat 27:28</u> And they stripped him, and put on him a **scarlet** robe. <u>Joh 19:2</u> And the soldiers platted a crown of thorns, and put *it* on his head, and they put on him a **purple** robe,

The color of Jesus' robe was? These could have been two different robes, a multi-colored robe, or as probably the case a scarlet robe that was used and then faded to resemble purple. The gospel writers wrote from their own perspectives. People perceive shades, tones, and tints differently.

223.<u>Mat 28:19</u> **Go ye therefore, and teach all nations,** baptizing them in the name of the Father, and of the Son, and of the Holy Ghost: <u>Mat 10:5</u> These twelve Jesus sent forth, and commanded them, saying, **Go not into the way of the Gentiles, and into *any* city of the Samaritans enter ye not:**

See 213.

224.<u>Mar 1:29</u> And forthwith, when they were come out of the synagogue, they entered into the house of Simon and Andrew, **with James and John.** <u>Mar 1:30</u> But Simon's wife's mother lay sick of a fever, and anon they tell him of her. <u>Luk 4:38</u> And he arose out of the synagogue, and entered into Simon's house. And Simon's wife's mother was taken with a great fever; and they besought him for her. <u>Luk 4:39</u> And he stood over her, and rebuked the fever; and it left her: and immediately she arose and ministered unto them.

Did James and John accompany Jesus to see Simon's mother? First of all, just because Luke does not mention them by name this doesn't mean they weren't there, secondly there is the word they mentioned in the passage which could be referring to them.

225.<u>Mar 5:2</u> And when he was come out of the ship, immediately there met him out of the tombs **a man** with an unclean spirit, <u>Mat 8:28</u> And when he was come to the other side into the country of the Gergesenes, **there met him two** possessed with devils, coming out of the tombs, exceeding fierce, so that no man might pass by that way.

How many people possessed? Mark simply doesn't mention both men.

226.<u>Mar 6:8</u> And commanded them that they should take nothing for *their* journey, **save a staff** only; no scrip, no bread, no money in *their* purse: <u>Luk 9:3</u> And he said unto them, Take nothing for *your* journey, **neither staves**, nor scrip, neither bread, neither money; neither have two coats apiece.

Were the disciples allowed to carry a staff? One is fine, but no more.

227.<u>Mar 7:26</u> The woman was **a Greek, a Syrophenician** by nation; and she besought him that he would cast forth the devil out of her daughter. <u>Mat 15:22</u> And, behold, **a woman of Canaan** came out of the same coasts, and cried unto him, saying, Have mercy on me, O Lord, *thou* Son of David; my daughter is grievously vexed with a devil.

Was the woman who has for Jesus' help a Greek or Canaanite? According to my source she was called a Canaanite because Matthew's target audience was Israel and because she was descended from the Canaanites. Mark called her Greek because she spoke it and called her a Syrophoenician because the lived in Phoenicia

https://christiancourier.com/articles/the-canaanite-woman-a-conflict-between-matthew-and-mark

228.<u>Mar 8:30</u> And he charged them that **they should tell no man of him**. <u>Joh 4:26</u> Jesus saith unto her, **I that speak unto thee am *he*.**

Did Jesus want to keep his Messiah-ship secret or not? Both are correct. Jesus' ministry lasted 3 years, he perhaps didn't want to let everybody know he was the Messiah up front early because it would have either caused him to go to the cross prematurely (before he had the chance to fill all those prophecies) or prevent the crucifixion altogether. Another possibility is that it depended on the circumstance or situation, it is Jesus' own discretion to whom he may make his self known to. In either case there is no contradiction. Jesus also made himself known to the man who was born blind (John 9:35-37). Jesus spoke in parables to keep things hidden from some (Matthew 13). Jesus also forbade devils to speak because they knew who he was (Mark 1:34).

229.<u>Mar 9:2</u> **And after six days** Jesus taketh *with him* Peter, and James, and John, and leadeth them up into an high mountain apart by themselves: and he was transfigured before them. <u>Luk 9:28</u> And it came to pass **about an eight**

days after these sayings, he took Peter and John and James, and went up into a mountain to pray. Luk 9:29 And as he prayed, the fashion of his countenance was altered, and his raiment *was* white *and* glistering.

Jesus was transfigured after six days or about eight? After six days is specific and about eight days is approximate therefore no contradiction. They are speaking of about the same time.

230.Mar 10:35 **And James and John**, the sons of Zebedee, come unto him, saying, Master, we would that thou shouldest do for us whatsoever we shall desire. Mat 20:20 Then came to him **the mother of Zebedee's children** with her sons, worshipping *him,* and desiring a certain thing of him.

Who asked Jesus for James and John to sit next to him in glory? They asked for themselves or their mama asked on their behalf? Just because Mark may have left the detail about their mom out of the equation it doesn't mean she didn't ask.

231.Mar 11:20 **And in the morning, as they passed by**, they saw the fig tree dried up from the roots. Mar 11:21 And Peter calling to remembrance saith unto him, Master, behold, the fig tree which thou cursedst is withered away. Mat 21:19 And when he saw a fig tree in the way, he came to it, and found nothing thereon, but leaves only, and said unto it, Let no fruit grow on thee henceforward for ever. **And presently the fig tree withered away.** Mat 21:20 And when the disciples saw *it,* they marvelled, saying, How soon is the fig tree withered away!

How soon did the fig tree wither? Immediately, the next day. The answer is that it started to wither immediately and was fully withered by the time they got back to it.

232.Mar 11:23 For verily I say unto you, That whosoever shall say unto this mountain, Be thou removed, and be thou cast into the sea; and shall not doubt in his heart, but shall believe that those things which he saith shall come to pass; **he shall have whatsoever he saith.** Mar 11:24 Therefore I say unto you, What things soever ye desire, when ye pray, believe that ye receive *them,* and ye shall have *them.* Jas 4:3 **Ye ask, and receive not**, because ye ask amiss, that ye may consume *it* upon your lusts.

Do we get whatever we pray for or are there restrictions? We get what we pray for if we are obedient (John 9:31), it's not sinful (Jas 4:3), and if it is according to God's will (1 John 5:14), oh and if we don't doubt (Jas 1:6-7).

233. <u>Mar 14:4</u> And **there were some that had indignation within themselves**, and said, Why was this waste of the ointment made? <u>Joh 12:4</u> Then saith **one of his disciples, Judas Iscariot**, Simon's *son,* which should betray him,

Who was mad about the ointment? What's the problem with Judas being among those that had indignation and John not mentioning the others in this passage?

234.<u>Mar 14:30</u> And Jesus saith unto him, Verily I say unto thee, That this day, *even* in this night, before the **cock crow twice,** thou shalt deny me thrice. <u>Mat 26:34</u> Jesus said unto him, Verily I say unto thee, That this night, before the **cock crow**, thou shalt deny me thrice.

How many times did the rooster crow after Peter denied Jesus. Once or twice? Mark wrote that Peter would deny Jesus three times before the cock crew twice, just because Matthew, Luke, and John omit this detail, this doesn't make a contradiction. The other gospels do not say that Peter would deny Jesus three times before the first crow or that the cock would only crow once.

235.<u>Mar 15:40</u> There were also women **looking on afar off**: among whom was Mary Magdalene, and Mary the mother of James the less and of Joses, and Salome; <u>Joh 19:25</u> **Now there stood by the cross** of Jesus his mother, and his mother's sister, Mary the *wife* of Cleophas, and Mary Magdalene.

Were the women close to or far away from the cross? People can move. Also their distance can be a matter of perspective.

236.<u>Mar 16:5</u> And entering into the sepulchre, they saw **a young man** sitting on the right side, clothed in a long white garment; and they were affrighted. <u>Luk 24:4</u> And it came to pass, as they were much perplexed thereabout, behold, **two men** stood by them in shining garments:

How many stood at the tomb? One or two? Once again, omitting a detail does not make a contradiction. A contradiction would say that only one man stood by the tomb.

237.<u>Mar 16:17</u> And these signs shall follow **them that believe**; In my name shall they cast out devils; they shall speak with new tongues; <u>Luk 9:49</u> And John answered and said, Master, we saw one casting out devils in thy name; and we forbad him, because **he followeth not with us.**

Is casting out devils a sign or a true believer? If the skeptic read the very next passage in Luke they would discover that this passage does not contradict the teaching of Mark 16. Let us consider Matthew 7:22-23 where we see that those who professed to follow Christ were said to cast out devils but ended up being lost, does this mean that you don't necessarily have to be saved to cast out devils? Maybe. But they could have been deceived and only thought that they were casting out devils, that is also a possibility. It's also possible that they cast out devils while they were walking with the Lord but then lost their salvation. We would do well to remember the sons of Sceva who for one reason or another attempted to drive out a demon using Jesus name but couldn't.

238.<u>Luk 1:41</u> And it came to pass, that, when Elisabeth heard the salutation of Mary, the babe leaped in her womb; and **Elisabeth was filled with the Holy Ghost**: <u>Joh 7:39</u> (But this spake he of the Spirit, which they that believe on him should receive: for **the Holy Ghost was not yet *given;*** because that Jesus was not yet glorified.)

When was the Holy Ghost given? Before or after the resurrection? The Holy Ghost is given in a more permanent and/or different sense after Jesus was raised. See gift of tongues in Acts 2, and Matthew 28 where Jesus says that he is always with us.

239.<u>Luk 3:23</u> And Jesus himself began to be about thirty years of age, being (as was supposed) the son of Joseph, which was ***the son* of Heli**, <u>Mat 1:16</u> And **Jacob begat Joseph** the husband of Mary, of whom was born Jesus, who is called Christ.

Who was Joseph's father? Jacob was the biological father, Heli was the father in law.

240.<u>Luk 4:40</u> Now when the sun was setting, all they that had any sick with divers diseases brought them unto him; and he laid his hands on **every one of them**, and healed them. <u>Mar 1:34</u> And he **healed many** that were sick of divers diseases, and cast out many devils; and suffered not the devils to speak, because they knew him.

Did Jesus heal many or all? If Jesus healed all then it can also mean he healed many.

241.<u>Luk 7:2</u> And a certain centurion's servant, who was dear unto him, was sick, and ready to die. <u>Luk 7:3</u> And when he heard of Jesus, **he sent unto him the elders of the Jews, beseeching him that he would come** and heal his servant. <u>Mat 8:5</u> And when Jesus was entered into Capernaum, **there came unto him a centurion**, beseeching him, <u>Mat 8:6</u> And saying, Lord, my servant lieth at home sick of the palsy, grievously tormented.

Did the centurion show up to Jesus personally or did he send others? He could have sent the Jews in his name.

242.<u>Luk 11:32</u> The men of Nineve shall rise up in the judgment with this generation, and shall condemn it: for they repented at the preaching of Jonas; and, behold, a **greater than Jonas *is* here**. <u>Mat 11:11</u> Verily I say unto you, Among them that are born of women there **hath not risen a greater than John the Baptist**: notwithstanding he that is least in the kingdom of heaven is greater than he.

Is Jesus greater than John? Jesus is greater because he is God, John was the greatest human prophet.

243.<u>Luk 14:26</u> If any *man* come to me, **and hate not his father, and mother, and wife,** and children, and brethren, and sisters, yea, and his own life also, he cannot be my disciple. <u>Lev 19:17</u> **Thou shalt not hate thy brother in thine heart:** thou shalt in any wise rebuke thy neighbour, and not suffer sin upon him.

Should we hate our family. Luke is using hyperbole to stress the fact that we should Love God so much that the love we have for our family would seem like hate by comparison, see Matthew 10:27.

244.<u>Luk 19:35</u> And they brought him to Jesus: and they **cast their garments upon the colt**, and they set Jesus thereon. <u>Joh 12:14</u> And Jesus, when **he had found a young ass**, sat thereon; as it is written,

Did Jesus sit on a colt or ass? The same animal.

245.<u>Luk 22:7</u> Then came the **day of unleavened bread,** when the passover must be killed. <u>Joh 13:1</u> Now **before the feast of the passover**, when Jesus knew that his hour was come that he should depart out of this world unto the Father, having loved his own which were in the world, he loved them unto the end.

When was the Lord's supper? Before or after the Passover? One thing to remember about Jewish time reckoning is the fact that the days starts at sunset. The evening and the morning were the 1ˢᵗ day, 2ⁿᵈ day etc (Genesis 1). There are multiple possible answers to this apparent contradiction, I will give just a few explanations that I've found during my research; but I will admit I do not know which is correct, there could be other explanations other than what is listed here.

1.) John may have been going by when the Sadducees were celebrating the Passover (they could have moved the day).

2.) Private home observances of the Passover meal could have been observed the evening before the public daytime one (still would be the same day by Jewish reckoning).

3.) The Passover may have been included in the days of unleavened bread.

246.<u>Luk 22:18</u> For I say unto you, I will not drink of the **fruit of the vine,** until the kingdom of God shall come. <u>Luk 22:19</u> **And he took bread**, and gave thanks, and brake *it,* and gave unto them, saying, This is my body which is given for you: this do in remembrance of me. <u>Mar 14:22</u> And as they did eat, **Jesus took bread**, and blessed, and brake *it,* and gave to them, and said, Take, eat: this is my body. <u>Mar 14:23</u> And **he took the cup**, and when he had given thanks, he gave *it* to them: and they all drank of it.

What was the order of the last supper? Drink then bread or vice versa? The order was Drink, bread, then drink, see Luke 22:20.

247.Luk 23:40 **But the other answering rebuked him**, saying, Dost not thou fear God, seeing thou art in the same condemnation? Mar 15:32 Let Christ the King of Israel descend now from the cross, that we may see and believe. And **they that were crucified with him reviled him.**

Did one or both thieves revile Jesus. Both did, one repented.

248.Joh 1:30 This is he of whom I said, After me cometh a man which is preferred before me: for **he was before me.** Luk 1:26 And **in the sixth month the angel Gabriel was sent** from God unto a city of Galilee, named Nazareth,

Who came first John or Jesus? Jesus existed as God before John, but took on flesh after John was conceived.

249.Joh 1:29 The next day John seeth Jesus coming unto him, and saith, **Behold the Lamb of God, which taketh away the sin of the world.** Mat 11:3 And said unto him, **Art thou he that should come,** or do we look for another?

Did John believe in Jesus? He did but doubted in prison.

250.Joh 3:22 After these things came **Jesus** and his disciples into the land of Judaea; and there he tarried with them, **and baptized.** Joh 4:2 (Though **Jesus himself baptized not**, but his disciples,)

Did Jesus baptize? His disciples baptized in his name.

251.Joh 6:17 And entered into a ship, and went over the sea **toward Capernaum**. And it was now dark, and Jesus was not come to them. Mar 6:53 And when they had passed over, they came into **the land of Gennesaret**, and drew to the shore.

Did the disciples sail to Capernaum or Gennesaret? The critic fails to read the text carefully they didn't go to Capernaum they went toward Capernaum, meaning in the general direction.

252.<u>Joh 8:14</u> Jesus answered and said unto them, **Though I bear record of myself,** *yet* **my record is true:** for I know whence I came, and whither I go; but ye cannot tell whence I come, and whither I go. <u>Joh 5:31</u> **If I bear witness of myself, my witness is not true.**

Is Jesus record true if he bears witness of himself? Just read two verses later in John 8 and you find out that Jesus is not alone; at the mouth of two witnesses shall every word be established (Matthew 18:16).

253.<u>Joh 11:26</u> And whosoever liveth and believeth in me **shall never die.** Believest thou this? <u>Heb 9:27</u> And as it is **appointed unto men once to die,** but after this the judgment:

Believers in Jesus don't die? All men are appointed a physical death, however spiritual death aka separation from God will not occur to believers.

254.<u>Joh 14:26</u> But the Comforter, *which is* the Holy Ghost, **whom the Father will send** in my name, he shall teach you all things, and bring all things to your remembrance, whatsoever I have said unto you. <u>Joh 15:26</u> But when the Comforter is come, **whom I will send** unto you from the Father, *even* the Spirit of truth, which proceedeth from the Father, he shall testify of me:

Who sends the comforter? Father or Jesus. They both do.

255.<u>Joh 17:12</u> While I was with them in the world, I kept them in thy name: those that thou gavest me I have kept, and **none of them is lost, but the son of perdition**; that the scripture might be fulfilled. <u>Joh 18:9</u> That the saying might be fulfilled, which he spake, Of them which thou gavest me **have I lost none.**

Judas wasn't given to Jesus to believe on him, Judas was chosen to fulfill the role of the betrayer, though it was by his own free will (Read, John 6:64-71).

256.<u>Joh 19:7</u> The Jews answered him, We have a law, and **by our law he ought to die,** because he made himself the Son of God. <u>Joh 18:31</u> Then said Pilate unto them, Take ye him, and judge him according to your law. The Jews therefore said unto him, **It is not lawful for us to put any man to death:**

Did the Jews have a reason to kill Jesus? The Jews thought Jesus violated the Torah and as such should be killed. However the Jews were under Roman rule so they didn't have the authority of capital punishment.

257. Joh 19:14 And it was the preparation of the passover, and **about the sixth hour**: and he saith unto the Jews, Behold your King! Mar 15:25 And **it was the third hour**, and they crucified him.

What hour was the crucifixion? One gospel records Roman time, the other gospel Jewish time.

258. Joh 20:1 The first *day* of the week cometh Mary Magdalene early, **when it was yet dark**, unto the sepulchre, and seeth the stone taken away from the sepulchre. Mar 16:2 And very early in the morning the first *day* of the week, they came unto the sepulchre **at the rising of the sun.**

When did the women arrive at the tomb? At dark or at sunrise? They could have visited the tomb more than once that day or headed out at dark and arrived at sunrise.

259. Joh 20:2 Then she runneth, and cometh to Simon Peter, and to the other disciple, whom Jesus loved, and saith unto them, They have taken away the Lord out of the sepulchre, and **we know not where they have laid him.** Mar 16:6 And he saith unto them, Be not affrighted: Ye seek Jesus of Nazareth, which was crucified: **he is risen; he is not here: behold the place where they laid him.**

Did the women believe in the resurrection? Again, it makes since that they visited the tomb at least twice that day.

260. Joh 20:30 And **many other signs truly did Jesus in the presence of his disciples,** which are not written in this book: Mar 8:12 And he sighed deeply in his spirit, and saith, Why doth this generation seek after a sign? verily I say unto you, **There shall no sign be given unto this generation.**

The faithless did not receive signs but the disciples did (Matthew 13:58).

261.<u>Joh 21:25</u> And there are also many other things which Jesus did, the which, if they should be written every one, I suppose that **even the world itself could not contain the books that should be written.** Amen. <u>Act 1:1</u> The former treatise have I made, O Theophilus, **of all that Jesus began both to do and teach,**

Could Jesus' miracles be numbered? The passage in Acts is not to be taken literally. Luke meant "all" as in some of each kind of things that Jesus did.

Chapter 6: Acts-Revelation

262.<u>Act 1:18</u> Now this man purchased a field with the reward of iniquity; and **falling headlong, he burst asunder in the midst**, and all his bowels gushed out. <u>Mat 27:5</u> And he cast down the pieces of silver in the temple, and departed, and went and **hanged himself.**

How did Judas die? By falling or hanging? Hanging, but his dead body fell down later and burst asunder.

263.<u>Act 2:4</u> And they were all **filled with the Holy Ghost,** and began to speak with other tongues, as the Spirit gave them utterance. <u>Joh 20:22</u> And when he had said this, he breathed on *them,* and saith unto them, **Receive ye the Holy Ghost:**

When was the Holy Ghost given? These are talking about different senses. According to my source the former verse was to provide power to be a witness and the latter was for salvation. It is believed by some that the indwelling of the Spirit is different from the baptism of the Spirit.

https://defendinginerrancy.com/bible-solutions/John_20.22.php

264.<u>Act 2:38</u> Then Peter said unto them, Repent, and be **baptized every one of you in the name of Jesus Christ** for the remission of sins, and ye shall receive the gift of the Holy Ghost. <u>Mat 28:19</u> Go ye therefore, and teach all nations, baptizing them **in the name of the Father, and of the Son, and of the Holy Ghost:**

What is the baptismal formula? Two possible answers. #1 Matthew is the biblical command but Acts is describing what happened. #2 Baptizing in Jesus name is baptizing in the name of the Father and Spirit (John 5:43, 14:26).

265.<u>Act 5:30</u> The God of our fathers raised up Jesus, whom ye slew and hanged on a **tree.** <u>Mat 27:40</u> And saying, Thou that destroyest the temple, and buildest *it* in three days, save thyself. If thou be the Son of God, come down from the **cross.**

Jesus hanged on what? Tree or cross? A Tree made from a cross.

266.<u>Act 7:6</u> And God spake on this wise, That his seed should sojourn in a strange land; and that they should bring them into bondage, and entreat *them* evil **four hundred years.** <u>Exo 12:41</u> And it came to pass at the end of the **four hundred and thirty years,** even the selfsame day it came to pass, that all the hosts of the LORD went out from the land of Egypt.

This could've been a subset fallacy if I didn't have some juicy details in store. After all 400 is a subset of 430. One author could have rounded to the nearest hundred while the other to the nearest ten. But wait...it gets better. The 430 years was referring to the time the promise was given to Abraham and the giving of the law to Israel (Galatians 3:16). A promise that was made two and a half decades before Isaac was born (Gen 12:1-4, 17:21-24). The 400 is in reference to Abraham's descendants, beginning with Isaac, dwelling in a land that is not theirs (Genesis 15:13).

267.<u>Act 7:14</u> Then sent Joseph, and called his father Jacob to *him,* and all his kindred, **threescore and fifteen souls.** <u>Gen 46:26</u> All the souls that came with Jacob into Egypt, which came out of his loins, besides Jacob's sons' wives, all the souls *were* **threescore and six;**

How many went with Jacob to Egypt? 66 or 75. Genesis wasn't counting the wives.

268.<u>Act 9:7</u> And the men which journeyed with him stood speechless, **hearing a voice**, but seeing no man. <u>Act 22:9</u> And they that were with me saw indeed the light, and were afraid; but they **heard not the voice of him** that spake to me.

A simple explanation is that they heard the sound of talking but perceived not what was spoken.

269.<u>Act 9:8</u> And Saul arose from the earth; and when his eyes were opened, **he saw no man**: but they led him by the hand, and brought *him* into Damascus. <u>1Co 9:1</u> Am I not an apostle? am I not free? **have I not seen Jesus Christ** our Lord? are not ye my work in the Lord?

Did Paul Jesus on the road to Damascus? Who says that Jesus appeared to Paul only once? The passage in Corinthians may not be referring to Paul's initial conversion.

270.<u>Act 13:21</u> And afterward they desired a king: and God gave unto them Saul the son of Cis, a man of the tribe of Benjamin, by the space of **forty years.** <u>1Sa 7:2</u> And it came to pass, while the ark abode in Kirjathjearim, that the time was long; for it was **twenty years**: and all the house of Israel lamented after the LORD.

How long was the Ark at Abinadab's house? 20 or 40 years? If the Ark was at Abinadab's house for forty years then by necessity is was there 20 years (plus 20 more). There is no text in the bible that says that the Ark wasn't already at Abinadabs house for twenty or more years when the events of 1 Samuel 7:2 began to occur.

271.<u>Act 16:31</u> And they said, Believe on the Lord Jesus Christ, and **thou shalt be saved, and thy house.** <u>1Co 7:16</u> For what knowest thou, O wife, whether thou shalt save *thy* husband? **or how knowest thou, O man, whether thou shalt save *thy* wife?**

Does believing in the gospel cause others to be saved? The disciples in the book of acts may have been prophesying what would happen rather than saying that the guards faith had to cause his families salvation.

272.<u>Act 22:11</u> And when **I could not see for the glory of that light**, being led by the hand of them that were with me, I came into Damascus. <u>Act 26:16</u> But rise, and stand upon thy feet: **for I have appeared unto thee for this purpose,** to make thee a minister and a witness both of these things which thou hast seen, and of those things in the which I will appear unto thee;

Did Saul see Jesus at the road to Damascus? Jesus did appear to Saul at the road to Damascus but Paul could not discern his form due to the light.

273.<u>Act 26:23</u> That Christ should suffer, *and* that he should be the **first that should rise from the dead**, and should shew light unto the people, and to the

Gentiles. <u>1Ki 17:22</u> And the LORD heard the voice of Elijah; and **the soul of the child came into him again**, and he revived.

Who was the first to be raise from the dead? Jesus or others? Jesus was the first to receive a glorified body (Immortal).

274.<u>Rom 4:3</u> For what saith the scripture? **Abraham believed God, and it was counted unto him for righteousness.** <u>Jas 2:21</u> Was not **Abraham our father justified by works,** when he had offered Isaac his son upon the altar?

Are we saved by faith or works? We are saved by true faith, the kind demonstrated by good works.

275.<u>Rom 5:10</u> For if, **when we were enemies**, we were reconciled to God by the death of his Son, much more, being reconciled, we shall be saved by his life. <u>Joh 15:13</u> Greater love hath no man than this, that a man **lay down his life for his friends.**

Did Jesus die for his friends or enemies? Jesus died for his enemies who would become his friends.

276.<u>Rom 5:12</u> Wherefore, as **by one man sin entered into the world,** and death by sin; and so death passed upon all men, for that all have sinned: <u>1Ti 2:14</u> And Adam was not deceived, **but the woman being deceived was in the transgression.**

Who caused the fall? Adam or Eve. Eve, but Adam is blamed because he is the head.

277.<u>Rom 7:12</u> Wherefore the **law *is* holy**, and the commandment holy, and just, **and good.** <u>Eze 20:25</u> Wherefore **I gave them also statutes *that were* not good,** and judgments whereby they should not live;

Is the law good? God's law is good (what Paul was referring to in Romans. Ezekiel is referring to God putting Israel man's laws since they wouldn't keep his laws.

278.<u>Rom 8:11</u> But if **the Spirit of him that raised up Jesus from the dead** dwell in you, he that raised up Christ from the dead shall also quicken your mortal bodies by his Spirit that dwelleth in you. <u>Joh 2:19</u> Jesus answered and said unto them, Destroy this temple, and in three days **I will raise it up.**

Who raised Jesus? All three members of the Godhead raised Jesus, see also Romans 6:4.

279.<u>Rom 11:26</u> And **so all Israel shall be saved:** as it is written, There shall come out of Sion the Deliverer, and shall turn away ungodliness from Jacob: <u>Mat 8:12</u> **But the children of the kingdom shall be cast out** into outer darkness: there shall be weeping and gnashing of teeth.

Shall all Israel be saved? Not all of the physical descendants of Abraham but all the household of faith shall be saved. Romans 2:28-29, 11:11-24, Gal 3:6-9).

280.<u>Rom 13:1</u> **Let every soul be subject unto the higher powers.** For there is no power but of God: the powers that be are ordained of God. <u>Act 5:29</u> Then Peter and the *other* apostles answered and said, **We ought to obey God rather than men.**

Should we obey the Law? Yes (1 Peter 2:13-14, Titus 3:1), unless it contradicts God's laws (Exodus 1, Daniel 1,3,6).

281.<u>Rom 15:33</u> Now the **God of peace** *be* with you all. Amen. <u>Exo 15:3</u> **The LORD** *is* **a man of war**: the LORD *is* his name.

Is God peaceful or warlike? Peaceful to his children but reigns vengeance on those who remain his adversaries.

282.<u>1Co 1:17</u> For **Christ sent me not to baptize,** but to preach the gospel: not with wisdom of words, lest the cross of Christ should be made of none effect. <u>Mat 28:19</u> Go ye therefore, and teach all nations, **baptizing them** in the name of the Father, and of the Son, and of the Holy Ghost:

Should Christian's baptize? Generally yes, but Jesus had other plans for Paul's ministry.

283.<u>1Co 2:8</u> Which **none of the princes of this world knew:** for had they known *it,* they would not have crucified the Lord of glory. <u>Mat 27:25</u> Then answered all the people, and said, **His blood *be* on us,** and on our children.

Did the people know who Jesus was? If they really believed Jesus was God/the Messiah, they probably wouldn't have condemned him in the Matthew reference.

284.<u>1Co 6:10</u> **Nor thieves,** nor covetous, nor drunkards, nor revilers, nor extortioners, **shall inherit the kingdom of God.** <u>Luk 23:43</u> And Jesus said unto him, Verily I say unto thee, **To day shalt thou be with me in paradise.**

Do thieves go to heaven? Repentant ones do that put their faith in Jesus.

285.<u>1Co 7:8</u> I say therefore to the unmarried and widows, **It is good for them if they abide even as I.** <u>Heb 13:4</u> **Marriage *is* honourable in all,** and the bed undefiled: but whoremongers and adulterers God will judge.

Is marriage good? Yes, marriage is good but staying single is better if you have the gift of celibacy. Read all of 1st Corinthians 7.

286.<u>1Co 8:4</u> As concerning therefore the eating of those things that are offered in sacrifice unto idols, we know that an idol *is* nothing in the world, and that ***there is* none other God but one.** <u>Psa 82:1</u> **A Psalm of Asaph.** God standeth in the congregation of the mighty; **he judgeth among the gods.**

How many gods are there? Is there only one God? There is only one true God, but many false ones.

287.<u>1Co 10:33</u> Even as **I please all *men* in all *things,*** not seeking mine own profit, but the *profit* of many, that they may be saved. <u>Gal 1:10</u> For do I now persuade men, or God? or do I seek to please men? for **if I yet pleased men, I should not be the servant of Christ.**

Should we please men or not? We should do good to all men (Galatians 6:10), but don't support them in their sin (1 Timothy 5:20).

288.<u>1Co 11:31</u> For **if we would judge ourselves, we should not be judged.** <u>1Co 4:3</u> But with me it is a very small thing that I should be judged of you, or of man's judgment: yea, **I judge not mine own self.**

Are Christian's to judge themselves? Yes we are to examine ourselves to see if we are in the faith (2 Corinthians 13:5), perhaps, what Paul is referring to in 1 Corinthians 4 is prognostication? In other words judging before the time. Or he could be referring to not judging himself by man's standards. These are just two possible solutions to this seeming contradiction, though they may not be a correct interpretation.

289.<u>1Co 14:39</u> Wherefore, brethren, **covet to prophesy,** and forbid not to speak with tongues. <u>Rom 13:9</u> For this, Thou shalt not commit adultery, Thou shalt not kill, Thou shalt not steal, Thou shalt not bear false witness, **Thou shalt not covet**; and if *there be* any other commandment, it is briefly comprehended in this saying, namely, Thou shalt love thy neighbour as thyself.

Is coveting a sin? It is a sin to covet your neighbors stuff because that is not loving them with your mind, however coveting spiritual gifts doesn't harm anyone.

290.<u>1Co 16:22</u> If any man love not the Lord Jesus Christ, let him be **Anathema Maranatha.** <u>Rom 12:14</u> Bless them which persecute you: bless, and **curse not.**

Should we curse others? Generally speaking, no. There are circumstances where we must cast out unruly "Christians" from the gathering until they repent for their good (1st Corinthians 5).

291.<u>2Co 6:14</u> **Be ye not unequally yoked together with unbelievers**: for what fellowship hath righteousness with unrighteousness? and what communion hath light with darkness? <u>1Co 7:13</u> And the woman which hath an husband that believeth not, and **if he be pleased to dwell with her, let her not leave him.**

Should Christian's marry unbelievers? No, however if they got married before he or she was a believer, or if the believer sinned and married them anyway, they should stay together unless the unbeliever leaves. If the unbeliever leaves some Christians teach the believer can divorce them.

292.<u>Gal 1:19</u> **But other of the apostles saw I none**, save James the Lord's brother. <u>Act 9:27</u> But Barnabas took him, and **brought *him* to the apostles,** and declared unto them how he had seen the Lord in the way, and that he had spoken to him, and how he had preached boldly at Damascus in the name of Jesus.

Did Paul see the other Apostles(besides Peter and James)? The passage in Acts does not say that Paul saw all the Apostles.

293.<u>Gal 3:13</u> Christ hath redeemed us from the curse of the law, being made a curse for us: for it is written, **Cursed *is* every one that hangeth on a tree:** <u>Act 5:30</u> The God of our fathers raised up **Jesus, whom ye slew and hanged on a tree.**

Is Jesus cursed? Jesus was made a curse for us when he took our place on the cross, but he didn't stay cursed.

294.*<u>Gal 4:10</u>* Ye observe days, and months, and times, and years. <u>Gal 4:11</u> I am afraid of you, lest I have bestowed upon you **labour in vain.** <u>Lev 23:4</u> **These *are* the feasts of the LORD,** *even* holy convocations, which ye shall proclaim in their seasons.

Is it wrong to celebrate Holy-days? It is wrong to celebrate Pagan festivals but the feast of the Lord are not pagan. You do not need to keep them physically to be saved though.

295.<u>Gal 5:2</u> Behold, I Paul say unto you, that **if ye be circumcised, Christ shall profit you nothing.** <u>Lev 12:3</u> And in the eighth day the flesh of his foreskin **shall be circumcised.**

Circumcision required? For Abraham and OT Israelites yes, New Testament Christians, no.

296.<u>Gal 5:4</u> Christ is become of no effect unto you, whosoever of you are justified by the law; **ye are fallen from grace.** <u>Rom 8:39</u> **Nor height, nor depth, nor any other creature, shall be able to separate us from the love of God,** which is in Christ Jesus our Lord.

Can one lose their salvation? Some believers say yes, others say no. My personal conviction on the matter is that one can forfeit their salvation through willful habitual sin. Note how the passage in Romans says any other creature, I don't believe that would include yourself. See 1 Corinthians 9:27, Hebrews 6,10, and 2 Peter 2:18-22.

297.<u>Gal 6:2</u> **Bear ye one another's burdens**, and so fulfil the law of Christ. <u>Gal 6:5</u> For every man shall **bear his own burden.**

We are to bear our own burdens and the burdens of those who cannot help themselves. Romans 15:1, 1 Thessalonians 5:14.

298.<u>Eph 3:8</u> Unto me, who am less than the **least of all saints,** is this grace given, that I should preach among the Gentiles the unsearchable riches of Christ; <u>2Co 12:11</u> I am become a fool in glorying; ye have compelled me: for I ought to have been commended of you: **for in nothing am I behind the very chiefest apostles,** though I be nothing.

Is Paul the least or greatest saint? Different senses Paul was the least of the saints because he persecuted the church, but once he was saved he labored more abundantly than the other Apostles (1 Corinthians 15:9-10).

299.<u>Eph 4:14</u> That we *henceforth* **be no more children,** tossed to and fro, and carried about with every wind of doctrine, by the sleight of men, *and* cunning craftiness, whereby they lie in wait to deceive; <u>Mat 18:3</u> And said, Verily I say unto you, **Except ye be converted, and become as little children, ye shall not enter into the kingdom of heaven.**

Being child-like is bad, or necessary to enter heaven. We should be humble like children and trust in our heavenly Father (believing his word), but we should not be gullible and believe everything we hear from men.

300.<u>Php 2:6</u> Who, being in the form of God, thought it **not robbery to be equal with God:** <u>Joh 14:28</u> Ye have heard how I said unto you, I go away, and come *again* unto you. If ye loved me, ye would rejoice, because I said, I go unto the Father: for **my Father is greater than I.**

Is Jesus equal with the Father or lesser than? Jesus has two natures. Divine and human, in his divinity he is equal to the Father.

301.<u>Php 2:27</u> For indeed he was sick nigh unto death: **but God had mercy on him**; and not on him only, but on me also, lest I should have sorrow upon sorrow. <u>Act 28:8</u> And it came to pass, that the father of Publius lay sick of a fever and of a bloody flux: to whom Paul entered in, and prayed, and **laid his hands on him, and healed him.**

Can believers heal others by laying hands on them? This is a topic that Christians are divided on. Some Christians believe in cessationism, which says some of the spiritual gifts ceased around the first century. continuationist believe we have access to all the spiritual gifts today. Some believe that the gift of healing does not guarantee 100% success, there was an instance where the disciples could not drive out a demon possessed boy (Mat 17). Though Jesus says it was because of their unbelief. Indeed, doubting can prevent healing (James 1:6-8).

302.<u>Col 2:13</u> And you, being dead in your sins and the uncircumcision of your flesh, hath he quickened together with him, having **forgiven you all trespasses;** <u>Mar 3:29</u> But he that shall blaspheme against the Holy Ghost hath **never forgiveness,** but is in danger of eternal damnation:

Is there an unforgivable sin? There are mixed opinions concerning the subject of the unforgivable sin. Matthew 12 and Luke 12 also deal with the subject of the unforgivable sin and say similar things. Some Christians say that it is impossible to commit this sin today because we do not have the amount of light that the pharisees had during their time (beholding Jesus in the flesh working miracles). <u>Some people teach that the blasphemy of the Spirit is rejecting Jesus for your entire life.</u> I personally am skeptical of these assertions. However the last point I made (the one underlined) would certainly show how these two passages are not contradictory (if this theory is true), since Colossians 2:13 is referring to believers. See also Acts 13:39 and 1 John 1:7,9).

303.<u>Col 3:25</u> But he that doeth wrong shall receive for the wrong which he hath done: and there is **no respect of persons.** <u>Exo 2:25</u> And God looked upon the children of Israel, and God had **respect unto *them.***

Does God respect persons? God does not show partiality or unfair favoritism in judgment he will punish those who sin, no matter who they are. But this is just one definition of the word respect, the other being to hold a person or action in honor or high esteem; this God does do.

304.<u>1Th 2:3</u> For our exhortation *was* not of deceit, nor of uncleanness, **nor in guile**: <u>2Co 12:16</u> But be it so, I did not burden you: nevertheless, being crafty, **I caught you with guile.**

A simple keyword search of the word guile shows that all verses unanimously condemning the sin of guile with the exception of 2 Corinthians 12:16, if I were to venture a guess here, I'd say that the Apostle Paul was being sarcastic here. A secondary howbeit less likely solution (I my opinion) is that the word guile has a secondary definition that isn't sinful (but I doubt it).

305.<u>1Th 5:21</u> **Prove all things**; hold fast that which is good. <u>1Co 13:7</u> Beareth all things, **believeth all things,** hopeth all things, endureth all things.

Should Christians believe everything? Christians should put full confidence in God (by what the bible says), but we should test the words of men (who are fallible).

306.<u>2Th 2:11</u> And for this cause **God shall send them strong delusion**, that they should believe a lie: <u>2Co 4:4</u> In whom the **god of this world** hath blinded the minds of them which believe not, lest the light of the glorious gospel of Christ, who is the image of God, should shine unto them.

Who blinds people from the truth of the Gospel? God or Satan? God can use Satan to punish unbelievers. Like Pharaoh, God can further harden the hearts of those who reject the gospel.

307.<u>1Ti 2:6</u> Who gave himself a **ransom for all,** to be testified in due time. <u>Mat 20:28</u> Even as the Son of man came not to be ministered unto, but to minister, and to give his life a **ransom for many.**

Did Christ die for everyone? Subset fallacy. If Christ Jesus died for all then he died for many.

308.2Ti 2:25 In meekness instructing those that oppose themselves; if **God peradventure will give them repentance** to the acknowledging of the truth; Act 17:30 And the times of this ignorance God winked at; but now **commandeth all men every where to repent:**

Who causes repentance? God gives men the ability to repent but the choice is up to them.

309.2Ti 3:16 **All scripture** *is* **given by inspiration of God**, and *is* profitable for doctrine, for reproof, for correction, for instruction in righteousness: 1Co 7:12 **But to the rest speak I, not the Lord**: If any brother hath a wife that believeth not, and she be pleased to dwell with him, let him not put her away.

Is all scripture inspired or just some? All scripture is inspired but not all scripture are commands.

310.Tit 1:2 In hope of eternal life, which **God, that cannot lie**, promised before the world began; Jer 4:10 Then said I, **Ah, Lord GOD! surely thou hast greatly deceived this people** and Jerusalem, saying, Ye shall have peace; whereas the sword reacheth unto the soul.

Can God lie? He can't, God is all good. However God can use the wicked to punish the wicked. The Lord suffered an evil spirit to cause prophets to lie in order to cause an Israelite king to fall in battle (1Kings 22).

311.Heb 1:4 **Being made so much better than the angels**, as he hath by inheritance obtained a more excellent name than they. Heb 2:9 But we see Jesus, who was **made a little lower than the angels** for the suffering of death, crowned with glory and honour; that he by the grace of God should taste death for every man.

Is Jesus greater or less than angels? Jesus has two natures in his divinity greater but since he became a man he was lesser in the sense that he could die.

312.Heb 7:3 Without father, **without mother**, without descent, having neither beginning of days, nor end of life; but made like unto the Son of God; abideth a priest continually. Gen 3:20 And Adam called his wife's name Eve; because she was the **mother of all living**.

Was Eve the mother of all living? She was the mother of all mankind, but Melchizedek was probably a pre-incarnate Christ, not just a man.

313.<u>Heb 8:1</u> Now of the things which we have spoken *this is* the sum: We have such **an high priest**, who is set on the right hand of the throne of the Majesty in the heavens; <u>Heb 10:10</u> By the which will we are sanctified through the **offering** of the body of Jesus Christ once *for all.*

Is Jesus the high priest or the offering? Both.

314.<u>Heb 9:4</u> Which had the golden censer, and the ark of the covenant overlaid round about with gold, w**herein *was* the golden pot that had manna, and Aaron's rod that budded, and the tables of the covenant**; <u>1Ki 8:9</u> *There was* nothing in the ark **save the two tables of stone,** which Moses put there at Horeb, when the LORD made *a covenant* with the children of Israel, when they came out of the land of Egypt.

Did the Ark contain the golden pot and Aaron's rod or just the tables? Things change with time the Ark at one time only had the tables and another time had the other items, or the items are put beside the Ark.

315.<u>Heb 9:27</u> And as it is appointed unto men **once to die**, but after this the judgment: <u>Gen 5:24</u> And Enoch walked with God: **and he *was* not;** for God took him.

Are all men destined to die, or do some get an exemption? In general most men will die as usual. Some men are changed by God and put on an immortal body, such as Enoch, Elijah, and those blessed to take part in the rapture.

316.<u>Heb 10:31</u> *It is* a **fearful thing** to fall into the hands of the living God. <u>2Sa 24:14</u> And David said unto Gad, I am in a great strait: let us fall now into the hand of the LORD; **for his mercies *are* great**: and let me not fall into the hand of man.

Is it fearful to fall into God's hands or not? It is fearful if you are disobedient and rebellious but not so if you are humble and repent of your evil.

317.<u>Heb 11:5</u> By **faith Enoch was translated that he should not see death**; and was not found, because God had translated him: for before his translation he had this testimony, that he pleased God. <u>Joh 3:13</u> And **no man hath ascended up to heaven,** but he that came down from heaven, *even* the Son of man which is in heaven.

Has any ascended into heaven? The short answer is either all the saved dead are in Abraham's bosom in a separate paradise chamber in hell or Jesus was saying nobody has went to heaven and came back to tell us what they saw (at least at that time).

318.<u>Jas 1:13</u> Let no man say when he is tempted, I am tempted of God: for God cannot be tempted with evil, **neither tempteth he any man**: <u>Gen 22:1</u> And it came to pass after these things, that **God did tempt Abraham**, and said unto him, Abraham: and he said, Behold, *here* I *am.*

Does God tempt people? God doesn't tempt people in the sense of enticing them to sin. However God does test the faithfulness of his followers.

319.<u>Jas 2:12</u> So speak ye, and so do, as they that shall be **judged by the law of liberty.** <u>Gal 4:24</u> Which things are an allegory: for these are the two covenants; the one from the mount Sinai, **which gendereth to bondage,** which is Agar.

Does the Law cause liberty or bondage? There are two different laws, the Mosaic law and the law of Christ. There is and old and new Testament. Romans 8:2,Galatians 6:2, Hebrews 7 and 8.

320.<u>Jas 2:25</u> Likewise also was not Rahab the harlot **justified by works**, when she had received the messengers, and had sent *them* out another way? <u>Heb 11:31</u> **By faith the harlot Rahab perished not** with them that believed not, when she had received the spies with peace.

Was Rahab justified by works or faith? Faith, that was proved by works.

321.<u>Jas 5:1</u> Go to now, *ye* **rich men, weep and howl** for your miseries that shall come upon *you.* <u>Pro 15:6</u> **In the house of the righteous *is* much treasure:** but in the revenues of the wicked is trouble.

Are righteous or wicked people rich or are riches bad? Riches are neutral, it's not about how much wealth you have, it's what your heart posture is about it, don't make money an idol. Don't serve mammon.

322.<u>1Pe 1:2</u> Elect according to the foreknowledge of God the Father, through **sanctification of the Spirit,** unto obedience and sprinkling of the blood of Jesus Christ: Grace unto you, and peace, be multiplied. <u>Joh 17:17</u> **Sanctify them through thy truth:** thy word is truth.

Are we sanctified by the Spirit or truth? Why not both?

323.<u>1Pe 1:4</u> To an inheritance incorruptible, and undefiled, and **that fadeth not away,** reserved in heaven for you, <u>Mat 24:35</u> **Heaven and earth shall pass away**, but my words shall not pass away.

Will our heavenly substance fade? No, our substance is in the 3rd heaven which is eternal. It is the first and possibly second heaven that will dissolve.

324.<u>1Pe 1:17</u> And if ye call on the **Father**, who without respect of persons **judgeth according to every man's work,** pass the time of your sojourning *here* in fear: <u>Joh 5:22</u> For the **Father judgeth no man**, but hath committed all judgment unto the Son:

Does the Father judge? Jesus and the Father are one (John 10:30), the Father's judgment would be in harmony with the Son's verdict.

325.<u>2Pe 2:4</u> For if God spared not the angels that sinned, but cast *them* down to hell, and **delivered *them* into chains of darkness**, to be reserved unto judgment; <u>Mat 12:22</u> Then was **brought unto him one possessed with a devil**, blind, and dumb: and he healed him, insomuch that the blind and dumb both spake and saw.

Are demons free to come and go as they please? There are devils and there are fallen angels? Are they one in the same? Maybe, maybe not. Who's to say there is only one category of fallen angel or devil. Why can't some be locked up (particularly the ones that supposedly mated with human women)and others not as restrained?

326.<u>1Jn 1:8</u> **If we say that we have no sin, we deceive ourselves,** and the truth is not in us. <u>1Jn 3:9</u> **Whosoever is born of God doth not commit sin;** for his seed remaineth in him: and he cannot sin, because he is born of God.

Do Christians sin? All have sinned but Christians do not make a habit of sinning, they fight against the parts of themselves that are yet to be like Jesus and strive to overcome the desires old man. Christians are taught to renew their mind (Romans 12:2), and are being shaped by God to be more like the Son (Romans 8:29, Galatians 4:19).

327.<u>1Jn 2:13</u> **I write unto you, fathers,** because ye have known him *that is* from the beginning. I write unto you, young men, because ye have overcome the wicked one. I write unto you, little children, because ye have known the Father. <u>Mat 23:9</u> **And call no *man* your father upon the earth:** for one is your Father, which is in heaven.

Can we call people father? We can call our earthly fathers father, but giving the context of Matthew 23 we are not to call men father in a religious context like the Catholics do.

328.<u>1Jn 3:8</u> **He that committeth sin is of the devil;** for the devil sinneth from the beginning. For this purpose the Son of God was manifested, that he might destroy the works of the devil. <u>1Ti 1:15</u> This *is* a faithful saying, and worthy of all acceptation, that Christ Jesus came into the world to save **sinners; of whom I am chief.**

Sinners are of the devil, Paul was the chief sinner? The difference is Paul repented and was adopted into the family of God, like all born again Christians.

329.<u>1Jn 4:2</u> Hereby know ye the Spirit of God: **Every spirit that confesseth that Jesus Christ is come in the flesh is of God:** <u>Mar 3:11</u> And unclean spirits, when they saw him, fell down before him, and cried, saying, Thou art the Son of God.

Those that confess Jesus are/are not of God. One explanation is that John was referring to a starting point in determining those that are of God. There are wolves in sheep's clothing y'know. Another explanation is that these are two different senses. John is referring to judging people (mankind), whereas Mark is describing an evil spirit.

330.Jud 1:9 Yet **Michael the archangel**, when contending with the devil he disputed about the body of **Moses**, durst not bring against him a railing accusation, but said, The Lord rebuke thee. Zec 3:1 And he shewed me **Joshua** the high priest standing before **the angel of the LORD**, and Satan standing at his right hand to resist him.

I'm just going to say these are describing two different events with different people. The angel of the Lord could be referring to Jesus here.

331.Jud 1:14 And Enoch also, the **seventh from Adam**, prophesied of these, saying, Behold, the Lord cometh with ten thousands of his saints, Luk 3:37 Which was *the son* of Mathusala, which was *the son* of Enoch, which was *the son* of Jared, which was *the son* of Maleleel, which was *the son* of Cainan, Luk 3:38 Which was *the son* of Enos, which was *the son* of Seth, which was *the son* of Adam, which was *the son* of God.

Was Enoch the sixth or the seventh from Adam? You are to count Adam, in which case it's seven.

332.Rev 5:5 And one of the elders saith unto me, Weep not: behold, **the Lion of the tribe of Juda**, the Root of David, hath prevailed to open the book, and to loose the seven seals thereof. Joh 1:29 The next day John seeth Jesus coming unto him, and saith, Behold **the Lamb** of God, which taketh away the sin of the world.

Is Jesus a lion or lamb? These are symbolic and describe different aspects of the messiah. Jesus is a spotless lamb in the sense that he is sinless and paid for our sins (Numbers 28:3). I would suppose that the lion represents his power (Proverbs 30:30) and regal birthright.

333.Rev 15:4 Who shall not fear thee, O Lord, and glorify thy name? **for thou only art holy:** for all nations shall come and worship before thee; for thy judgments are made manifest. Lev 19:2 Speak unto all the congregation of the children of Israel, and say unto them, **Ye shall be holy:** for I the LORD your God *am* holy.

Is only God holy? Only God is perfectly holy in the sense that he never has sinned and completely distinct from creation. We however are to be holy through the power and indwelling of the Holy Spirit.

334.<u>Rev 19:15</u> And out of his mouth goeth a sharp sword, that with it he should smite the nations: and he shall rule them with a rod of iron: and **he treadeth the winepress of the fierceness and wrath of Almighty God.** <u>Luk 9:56</u> For the Son of man is **not come to destroy men's lives, but to save** *them.* And they went to another village.

Did Jesus come to save or destroy? Jesus has two comings. The first to save, the second to destroy and set up his perfect kingdom.

Chapter 7: Bible Version Issue Introduction

For this chapter I will be giving the reader a brief overview of the bible version controversy. While I personally do not Identify as a KJV-onlyist, I do believe it is the best version for the English speaking people. I take on faith that is the closest to the Hebrew and Greek Manuscripts. I do not teach or believe that one must read the KJV to be a Christian, nor do I think that one should divide over this issue. However I do believe that there are some serious changes made to newer bibles that do affect doctrine and could lead some astray.

Again, I want to stress that this is a brief summary of the KJV Issue as the goal of this book is to examine and expose as many bible corruptions as possible in a very short space, therefore I will not be giving an exhaustive account of the history of this issue. For an exhaustive account of the KJV vs Modern bible issue, I suggest checking out Chick Tracts Official YouTube Channel, or av.1611.com.

One last thing before we continue, I'd just like to state that although I use the site creation liberty as a reference this does not mean that I'm in agreement with Christopher Johnson's view on repentance. I believe repentance does mean to turn from sin as well as godly sorrow.

Translation Types

Before going any further in this issue, I find it helpful to briefly describe the various kind of bibles out there. Out of the dozens (if not hundreds), of English bibles to choose from there are just three types of bibles. There is the word for word translations (my personal favorite), the thought for thought translations, and paraphrases.

Word for word Translations- Carry over the wording from the Hebrew and Greek into English, they are literal translations and I deem them more trustworthy for doctrine and accuracy.

- King James

- New King James

- Young Literal Translation

- Revised Standard

- American Standard

- New American Standard

Thought for thought Translations - Or dynamic equivalence tries to capture the meaning of the text or what the original author intended (may not use the precise wording).

- New International Version

- English Standard Version

- Contemporary English Version

- Good News Bible

Paraphrase - Although created for easy reading and considered more modern, these bibles cannot be trusted to decipher the meaning of the text and therefore I would not recommend to anyone.

- The Living Bible

- The Message

- The word on the Street (I added this one, not in link)

https://bibleanswers.study/about-the-bible/types-of-bible-versions

<u>The Majority vs. The Minority Text</u>

Now that we have briefly covered the types of bibles available out there, now we are going to go over an important point in the bible version controversy, and that is the majority vs minority text.

The majority text is also called the traditional text, the Antioch text, the received text, among other titles. It is represented by over 5000 manuscripts. These text agree with each other.

On the other hand the minority text (also called the Alexandrian text) only make up about 1% of the manuscripts and are in disagreement in many places. Perhaps the two most famous manuscripts of this category is the codex Vaticanus and Sinaticus (which we shall cover shortly).

I personally do not consider myself a KJV-ONLYist (though that is the only translation I read, unless covering this topic), I'd rather consider myself a Majority text believer. Because of the doctrine of preservation (which can be found in my 1st book Bible Verses for Born-Again Believers Vol 1), I believe that the majority text is the best reading to follow.

The main argument used for trusting the minority text is because they are supposedly older (and therefore believed to be less likely corrupted) text. I personally do not like this line of reasoning on two counts. For one just because something is older it doesn't mean it hasn't been corrupted for there were many which corrupted the word in Paul's day (2 Corinthians 2:17), and secondly when something is used a lot it wears out. So it stands to reason that the oldest manuscripts (if Sinaiticus and Vaticanus really are the oldest) lasted so long because people knew they were tainted and therefore didn't read them.

Alexandria Vs Antioch

Once notable difference between the majority and the minority text is the location of their source. The majority text come from Antioch (which is mentioned positively in scripture), while the minority text come from Alexandria, Egypt; which often has a negative connotation. Consider the following few example. For more examples I suggest a keyword search.

Jdg 6:8 That the LORD sent a prophet unto the children of Israel, which said unto them, Thus saith the LORD God of Israel, I brought you up from Egypt, and brought you forth out of the house of bondage;

2Ki 18:21 Now, behold, thou trustest upon the staff of this bruised reed, *even* upon Egypt, on which if a man lean, it will go into his hand, and pierce it: so *is* Pharaoh king of Egypt unto all that trust on him.

Isa 19:14 The LORD hath mingled a perverse spirit in the midst thereof: and they have caused Egypt to err in every work thereof, as a drunken *man* staggereth in his vomit.

Jer 42:17 So shall it be with all the men that set their faces to go into Egypt to sojourn there; they shall die by the sword, by the famine, and by the pestilence: and none of them shall remain or escape from the evil that I will bring upon them.

Eze 29:3 Speak, and say, Thus saith the Lord GOD; Behold, I *am* against thee, Pharaoh king of Egypt, the great dragon that lieth in the midst of his rivers, which hath said, My river *is* mine own, and I have made *it* for myself.

Act 11:26 And when he had found him, he brought him unto Antioch. And it came to pass, that a whole year they assembled themselves with the church, and taught much people. And the disciples were called Christians first in Antioch.

Act 11:27 And in these days came prophets from Jerusalem unto Antioch.

Act 15:35 Paul also and Barnabas continued in Antioch, teaching and preaching the word of the Lord, with many others also.

Vaticanus and Sinaiticus

The two most prominent minority text manuscripts of the bible version issue are Codex's Sinaiticus and Vaticanus. Therefore if they can be shown to be untrustworthy it would be a substantial blow to the many modern bibles which sprung up as a result of them. So the question is can we trust codex Sinaticus and Vaticanus? The answer is a resounding no. Here are just a few reasons to doubt the integrity of the two codexs.

"The impurity of the text exhibited by these codices is not a question of opinion but fact...In the Gospels alone, Codex B (Vatican) leaves out words or whole clauses no less than 1,491 times. It bears traces of careless transcriptions on every page.

– John W. Burgon, quoted by Larry Alavezos, A Primer on Salvation and Bible Prophecy, TEACH Services Inc., 2010, p. 84-85, ISBN: 9781572586406

"It should be noted... that there is no prominent Biblical (manuscripts) in which there occur such gross cases of misspelling, faulty grammar, and omission, as in (Codex) B."

-Henry S. Gehman & John D. Davis, The New Westminster Dictionary of the Bible, Westminster Press, 1970; See also Supplement to the Journal of the American Oriental Society, American Oriental Society, Vol. 59, 1939, p. 264

Although the following sites may not have all the detailed references of the last two quotes they are still worth checking out as they explain the bible version a lot more fully than I will provide in this publication

https://www.bibleready.org/modern-translations

https://www.chick.com/information/article?id=bible-texts

https://www.1611kingjamesbible.com/codex_vaticanus.html/

In regards to the other codex (Sinaticus) it was found by Tischendorf in the Mount Sinai monastery, it took him three trips to fully recover it. It is said to have come from the around the 4th Century A.D. The problem with that is that a contemporary of Tishcendorf (Simonides) claimed to have written the codex. Simonides made it as a gift for the Russian Tzar, in the hope he would bestow upon the monastery a printing press.

However shortly before it was finished it disappeared, only to be found by Tishchendorf. To support his claim Simonides named several distinct marks on various pages of the manuscript, however those parts of the work mysteriously disappeared. Simonides perished under puzzling circumstances not long after. A friend of Simonides proclaimed that he saw Tishcendorf treating the pages of the codex with lemon juice (claiming to be cleaning them). Lemon juice makes paper look older than it actually is.

https://www.godsessions.com/battle-for-the-bible

<u>Beware the Jesuits!</u>

I'm quite confident that most of my readers have heard of the protestant reformation which took place on October 31st 1517. What I'm also quite confident in is that relatively few people are aware of the Catholic counter-reformation. Now I'll admit that I've hadn't done a lot of research on the Jesuits myself and so I do not have a lot to say on the matter, I will however list a few facts/quotes in order to perhaps whet my readers appetite in the hopes that they will delve deeper into the topic elsewhere.

Some may call me a conspiracy theorist, but I care not; I do believe the Jesuits are at least partly responsible for a considerable portion of our Newer Translations. Consider the following. It used to be considered a crime for a layperson to read the bible for themselves centuries ago. It is a well recorded fact that protestants were tortured and killed by Catholics for their beliefs. Does anyone expect me to believe that the Jesuits gave up once the bible was no longer outlawed?

According to <u>Britannica</u> the society of Jesus (Jesuits) were referred to as the "shock troops" of the counter reformation. Here are two quotes that should convince anyone that the Jesuits should not be trusted in translating the bible.

https://www.britannica.com/biography/Pius-IV

Here is part of the Jesuit oath that was made public back in in 1883 but is still in force presently.

"I furthermore promise and declare that I will, when opportunity presents, make and wage relentless war, secretly or openly, against all heretics, Protestants and Liberals, as I am directed to do, to extirpate and exterminate them from the face of the whole earth; and that I will spare neither age, nor sex or condition; and that I will hang, burn, waste, spoil, flay, strangle, and bury alive these infamous heretics, rip up the stomachs and wombs of their women and crush their infants' heads against the walls, in order to annihilate forever their execrable race.

That when the same cannot be done openly, I will secretly use the poisoned cup, the strangulating cord, the steel of the poinard or the leaden bullet, regardless of the honor, rank, dignity, or authority of the person or persons, whatever may be their condition in life, either public or private, as I at any time may be directed to do so by any agent of the Pope or Superior of the Brotherhood of the Holy Faith, of the Society of Jesus."

https://endtimemessage.info/jesuit_order.html

"Then the Bible, (that serpent which with head erect and eyes flashing, threatens us with its venom while it trails along the ground), shall be changed into a rod as soon as we are able to seize it... for three centuries past this cruel asp has left us no repose. You well know with what folds it entwines us and with what fangs it gnaws us." – from a Jesuit meeting in Cheri, Italy in 1825, (The Jesuits in History, Hector Macpherson, Ozark Book Publishers, 1997, Appendix 1).

https://www.godsessions.com/battle-for-the-bible

I see no reason to doubt that the Jesuits are responsible for attacking the word of God. The bible tells us the following.

Mat 7:15 Beware of false prophets, **which come to you in sheep's clothing**, but inwardly they are ravening wolves.

Eph 6:12 For we wrestle not against flesh and blood, but against principalities, against powers, **against the rulers of the darkness of this world, against spiritual wickedness in high** *places*.

1Jn 4:1 Beloved, believe not every spirit, but try the spirits whether they are of God: because **many false prophets are gone out into the world.**

1Jn 5:19 *And* we know that we are of God, and the **whole world lieth in wickedness.**

The bible says that we will know them by their fruit, there is so much wickedness in this world and especially in the government, and big corporations. There is the FDA with it's poisonous foods and drugs, the public education system with it's indoctrination and LGBTQ agenda, the many false religions out there, and on and on it goes.

Wescott and Hort Vs The KJV Translators

Brooke F. Wescott and Fenton John Anthony Hort were the two men responsible for the Greek New Testament that underlies many, if not all of the modern bibles. The point I want to make in this section is that in terms of translator quality; the KJV translators were far more qualified to translate the bible than Wescott and Hort. Consider the following.

"No one now, I suppose, holds that the first three chapters of Genesis, for example, give a literal history—I could never understand how any one reading them with open eyes could think they did—yet they disclose to us a Gospel."

-Brooke F. Westcott, *Life and Letters of Brooke Foss Westcott*, Vol. 2, Macmillan and Company, 1903, p. 68-69

"I have been trying to recall my impressions of La Salette. I wish I could see to what **forgotten truth Mariolatry bears witness**; and how we can practically set forth the teaching of miracles."

-Brooke F. Westcott, *Life and Letters of Brooke Foss Westcott*, Vol. 2, Macmillan, 1903, p. 251, retrieved May 1, 2024, [https://archive.org/details/ LifeAndLettersOfBrookeFossWestcottVol1/page/n283/mode/1up]

"Nor, as far as I can recollect, have you anywhere written explicitly upon this point; even on the corresponding subject of vicarious righteousness I know only of two pages (Kingdom of Christ, 1st edition, vol. i. pp. 32, 33), and they have not been able to make me feel assured that the language of imputation is strictly true, however sanctioned by St. Paul's example. The fact is, **I do not see how God's justice can be satisfied without every man's suffering in his own person the full penalty for his sins.**"

-Fenton J.A. Hort, *Life and Letters of Fenton John Anthony Hort*, Macmillan, Vol. 1, 1896, p. 120, [University of Michigan]

Note: I removed the bracketed section of what I perceived to be Christopher's comments in the last quote.

"I am not able to go as far as you in asserting the absolute infallibility of a canonical writing.

-Fenton J.A. Hort, *Life and Letters of Fenton John Anthony Hort*, Macmillan, Vol. 1, 1896, p. 422, [University of Michigan]

https://www.creationliberty.com/articles/kingjames.php

Consider just a few of the accomplishments of the men who translated the KJV.

- **John Bois** (who was one of the twelve who made the last revision at Stationers Hall) at the tender age of five has read the entire bible, in Hebrew, and by the age of six could write Hebrew very well.

- **Lancelot Andrews** made his own private devotion manual, not impressive enough? Well he made it in Greek. He was also conversant in over a dozen languages.

- **Andrew Downes** was a Cambridge Greek Professor for forty years.

"Defending the King James Bible A Four Fold Superiority:" D.A. Waite pgs. 73, 67-68, 79

<u>KJV Editions Changes</u>

Some people may point out that even the KJV has had changes to it since it's creation over four hundred years ago, though true, what kind of changes are we talking about and how many? In terms of quantity there has only been 421 word changes in the KJV. That is approximately 1/500th of 1 percent of the text. That is a very small amount of changes. But what kind of changes are there? Are they serious. I will give a few example of the kind of changes that occurred in the various editions of the KJV and let the reader decide.

1. Lift to Lifted (51x)

2. Amongst to Among (36x)

3. You to ye (82x)

4. Burnt to Burned (31x)

Out of the 421 changes in the KJV about 300 of them are these kind of changes. So what about the remaining 100+? They are minor phrase changes such as cheweth cud being changed to cheweth the cud (Lev 11:3) or and wood changed to and the wood (Gen 22:7).

https://bible.org/article/changes-kjv-1611-illustration

Update: Upon further study of this topic I have come across some rather significant differences between some KJV editions. While I used to hold to the notion that the KJV was the inerrant word of God, today I cannot accept it at true; at least not for all editions. Do I love the KJV? Yes, absolutely. I still believe it's the best English version out there; but I can no longer claim 100% confidence that there is an error free KJV bible out there. Here are six examples of differences between or errors in KJV bibles.

AV 1611 vs. Modern KJV

- Jer 38:16 "So the king sware secretly" "So Zedekiah the king sware secretly"

- Jer 49:1 why then doth their king inherit…"God" "Gad"

- 1 Tim 1:4 "rather than edifying" "rather than godly edifying"

https://petergoeman.com/errors-in-king-james-version-kjv/

Worst KJV Changes/ Misprints

- "Thou shalt commit adultery…" 1631 Edition (Exodus 20:14)

- "Sin on more…" 1716 Edition (Jeremiah 31:34).

• "Let the children first be killed..." London issued 1795 KJV (Mark 7:27)

https://record.adventistchurch.com/2019/12/18/the-ten-worst-biblical-typos-of-all-time/

<u>Was King James gay?</u>

Sometimes in a KJV vs Modern Version discussion people may bring up the accusation that King James was gay (there is even a Queen James Bible to this effect), however the claim that James was gay is indeed false. Consider the following quotes.

"There appears a certain natural goodness verging on modesty... among his good qualities none shines more brightly than the chasteness of his life, which he has preserved without stain down to the present time, contrary to the example of almost all his ancestors, who disturbed the kingdom with the great number of bastards which they left."

-Henry Wotton, quoted by Stephen A. Coston & Richard D. Neumeier, *King James, the VI of Scotland & the I of England: Unjustly Accused?*, KonigsWort, 1996, p. 39, ISBN: 9780965677738

"...But especially eschew [i.e. hate] to be effeminate in your clothes, in perfuming, preining, or such like... And make not a fool of yourself in disguising or wearing long your hair or nails, which are but excrements of Nature [i.e. that which is discharged from the body] and betray such misusers of them, to be either of a vindictive, or a vain light nature;"

-King James I of England, *Basilikon Doron: His Majesty's Instructions to His Dearest Son, Henry the Prince*, Edinburgh, 1599, p. 132-133, published Wertheimer, Lea & Co., 1887, Cornell University Library, retrieved Aug 8, 2023, [https://archive.org/details/cu31924097402626/page/n181/mode/2up]

"But as this severe justice of yours upon all offenses would be but for a time (as I have already said), so is there some horrible crimes that ye are bound in Conscience never to forgive: such as Witchcraft, wilfull murder, Incest, (especially within the degrees of consanguinity [relationship by blood]) Sodomy, poisoning, and false coin:

-King James I of England, *Basilikon Doron: His Majesty's Instructions to His Dearest Son, Henry the Prince*, Edinburgh, 1599, p. 37-38, published Wertheimer, Lea & Co., 1887, Cornell University Library, retrieved Aug 8, 2023, [https://archive.org/details/cu31924097402626/page/n85/mode/2up]

https://www.creationliberty.com/articles/kingjames.php

Least Effective Bible Translation or Paraphrase Variations

The following is a list of Translation and/or Paraphrase Variations that probably will not be effective in persuading someone to switch from a newer translation to the KJV. Nevertheless they are listed here simply to show that various translations indeed say different things, although there are some change in meanings in these examples they are not the worst changes that I have came across, that is saved for Chapter 9. Some of these differences *may* not even be considered bad, but I've included them nonetheless. The KJV rendering is on the left (if included), and the newer version, most of the time will be on the right (and will also be in bold).

1. Gen 7:1 <u>Come</u> *changed to* "...**Go into the ark...**" (DBY) see also NASB95 for another change.
2. Gen 30:27 <u>experience</u> *changed to* "...**divined...**"(ASV).
3. Exodus 8:17 <u>lice</u> *changed to* "**insects**" (BBE) see also what the NLT says.
4. Exodus 14:25 <u>took off</u> *changed to* "...**stiff...**" (BBE) see also what the NLT, RSV, NASB20 states.
5. Exo 26:14 <u>badgers' skins</u> *changed to* "**sealskins**" (ASV) see also NLT
6. Leviticus 11:30 "...**gecko...land crocodile...chameleon.**" (ASV) Different animals listed.
7. Numbers 4:8 "...**sealskin...**" (ASV) See point #5.
8. Num 7:26 <u>spoon</u> *changed to* "**cup**" (DBY) see also the variations of the NKJV, NLT, HNV, RSV.
9. Num 11:5 "...**the fruit and green plants of every sort...**"(BBE). Not

as specific.

10. Num 17:8 <u>almonds</u> *changed to* "...**fruit**." (BBE).

11. Num 24:8 <u>unicorn</u> *changed to* "...**wild-ox**." (ASV)

12. Deuteronomy 7:20 <u>hornet</u> *changed to* "...**Locust**..." (YLT)

13. Deuteronomy 33:2 <u>fiery law</u> *changed to* "...**[are] springs**..." (YLT).

14. Judges 4:18 <u>mantle</u> *changed to* "...**rug**." (ASV)

15. Judges 14:15 <u>seventh day</u> *changed to* "...**fourth day**..." (BBE)

16. Judges 15:4 <u>foxes</u> *changed to* "...**jackals**..." (DARBY)

17. Judges 19:2 <u>played the whore against</u> *changed to* "...**was angry with him**..." (BBE)

18. 1 Samuel 5:9 <u>emerods</u> *changed to* "...**tumors**..." (ASV)

19. 1 Samuel 13:1 <u>Saul reigned one year</u> *changed to* "...***forty* years**..." (ASV) see also NLT for another rendering.

20. 2 Samuel 13:18 *garment of divers colours changed to* "...**had on a long robe**..."(BBE)

21. 2 Samuel 21:8 <u>Michal</u> *changed to* "...**Merab**..." (BBE)

22. 2 King 2:24 <u>children</u> *changed to* "...**lads**." (ASV)

23. Ezra 1:9 <u>knives</u> *changed to* "**platters**" (ASV) see also NASB95, NLT, NIV. For other translations.

24. Nehemiah 4:23 "...**every one *went with* his weapon to the water**." (ASV)

25. Job 1:11 "...**I pray Thee**..." (YLT)

26. Prov 18:24 <u>A man *that hath* friends must shew himself friendly</u> *changed to* "**A man of many friends will come to ruin**..."(BBE)

27. Prov 30:31 <u>greyhound</u> *changed to* "**The war-horse**..." (BBE)

28. Ecc 11:5 <u>spirit</u> *changed to* "...**wind**..." (ASV)

29. SOS 8:6 <u>jealousy</u> *changed to* "...**wrath bitter as the underworld**..." (BBE)

30. SOS 8:7 <u>it would</u> *changed to* "...**He would**..." (ASV)

31. Isaiah 1:18-20 <u>reason together</u> *changed to* "...**let us have an argument together**..." (BBE)

32. Lam 4:3 <u>sea monsters</u> *changed to* "...**jackals**..." (ASV)

33. Daniel 3:25 <u>Son of God</u> *changed to* "...**a son of the gods**." (ASV)

34. Hosea 3:1 <u>wine</u> *changed to* "...**grape-cakes**." (BBE)

35. Hos 8:14 <u>temples</u> *changed to* "...**palaces**..." (ASV)

36. Joel 1:4 **"worm, locust, plant-worm, field fly"** (BBE)
37. Joel 2:14 **"an oblation"**(DBY)
38. Matthew 28:19 <u>teach all nations</u> *changed to* "...**make disciples...**" (ASV)
39. Mat 28:20 <u>end of the world</u> *changed to* "...**completion of the age**". (DBY)
40. John 3:7 <u>Ye must be born again</u> *changed to* "...**It is necessary for you...**'" (BBE)
41. John 14:2 <u>mansions</u> *changed to* "...**abodes...**" (DBY)
42. Acts 5:11 <u>church</u> *changed to* "...**assembly...**" (DBY)
43. Acts 12:4 <u>Easter</u> *changed to* "...**Passover...**" (DBY)
44. Romans 6:22 "...**bondmen...**" (DBY) We choose to serve Christ, it's a choice we must make each day.
45. Galatians 3:13 <u>hangeth</u> *changed to* "...**hanged upon...**" (DBY). Wrong tense.
46. Philippians 3:8 <u>dung</u> *changed to* "...**refuse...**" (ASV)
47. Collosians 3:21 <u>provoke not your children *to anger*</u> *changed to* "**Fathers, do not be hard on your children...**"(BBE)
48. 1 Tim 5:14 <u>women</u> *changed to* "...**younger widows marry,...**" (ASV)
49. 2 Timothy 3:17 <u>perfect</u> *changed to* "...**complete,...**" (ASV)
50. Rev 11:8 <u>our Lord</u> *changed to* "...**their Lord was crucified**" (ASV).

Chapter 8: KJV Bonuses

In this chapter we will be taking a look at seventy examples of words, phrases, and/or verses that appear in the KJV but not necessarily in other versions, for this reason I will call this chapter KJV bonuses. There are at least a couple of reasons as to why the KJV has these bonus words in scripture. One reason is because the KJV translators added words (in italics) in order to make sense of the passage, they did this because those words were not in the manuscripts that they had at that time. This shows their honesty.

Another reason there are extra words in the KJV is because of the divided opinion among Christian scholars on whether or not certain passages (including the ending of Mark 16 for example) appeared in the original manuscripts, obviously the KJV translators did believe that what the case. For this section I am going to **BOLD** the words that appear in the KJV but not some other translations, and give my comments (if any) in *italics*.

1. 1 Samuel 6:19 omits "...**fifty thousand**..."(DBY)

This is a huge discrepancy in the number of men that were killed.

2. Prov 16:31 "*if*"

This is supposed to be a conditional statement, but is done away with the removal of one word.

3. Lamentations 3:26 removed **"hope"** (RSV)

See Romans 8:24 for why this is important.

4. Hosea 4:11 REMOVED **"whoredom"** (RSV)

5. Habbakuk 2:4 omits "**which is lifted up**" (RSV)

The KJV shows why a persons soul is not upright in him (pride), you lose that meaning in this bogus translation.

6. Nahum 1:10 removed **"and while they are drunken *as* drunkards,"**(RSV)

7. Matthew 1:25 **"firstborn"**

Was this omitted to enforce the Catholic dogma that Mary was a perpetual virgin?

8. Matthew 5:22 removes **"without a cause"**

There is such thing as righteous indignation, this change makes Jesus a sinner (Mark 3:5).

9. Mat 5:44 removes **"do good to them that hate you,"**

A difficult command for the unregenerate to follow, why would this be left out?

10. Mat 6:13 **"For thine is the kingdom, and the power, and the glory, for ever. Amen. "**

A very good ending to prayer, was this really not in the original? I think it was there.

11. Mat 9:13 **"to repentance"**

Removal of an essential biblical command!

12. Matthew 17:21 **"Howbeit this kind goeth not out but by prayer and fasting."**

An important verse for spiritual warfare, I can see why the enemy doesn't want you to know this.

13. Matthew 18:11 **"For the Son of man is come to save that which was lost. "**

14. Mat 19:19 **"and whoso marrieth her which is put away doth commit adultery."**

I can see why some people would want to remove this verse.

15. Mat 20:16 **"for many be called, but few chosen. "**

An important nugget of truth about salvation, few obtain it.

16. Matthew 23:14 **"Woe unto you, scribes and Pharisees, hypocrites! for ye devour widows' houses, and for a pretence make long prayer: therefore ye shall receive the greater damnation. "**

Could the Catholics have removed this because it condemns their priest for taking money from widows for there prayers for the departed. I'm going to say for one more time,...for! A little humor never hurt anyone right?

17. Mark 6:11 **" Verily I say unto you, It shall be more tolerable for Sodom and Gomorrha in the day of judgment, than for that city. "**

18. Mark 7:17 **"And when he was entered into the house from the people, his disciples asked him concerning the parable."**

19. Mark 9:44 **"Where their worm dieth not, and the fire is not quenched."**

20. Mark 9:46 **"Where their worm dieth not, and the fire is not quenched."**

A lot of people do not like the doctrine of hell, it could be hard for some people to swallow why a loving God would punish people forever for a limited amount of sins. While I'm not going to open that can of worms here, I will say that I fully believe in the reality of hell and that this verse should be here.

21. Mark 10:24 **"for them that trust in riches"**

22. Mark 10:21 "**take up the cross**"

The command to deny oneself is seen elsewhere in scripture (Matthew 16:34,Mark 8:34, Luke 9:23, 14:27). Nevertheless, it would be wrong to omit this phrase if it was in the originals.

23. Mark 11:26 "**But if ye do not forgive, neither will your Father which is in heaven forgive your trespasses.**"

Unforgiveness will send people to hell.

24. Mark 15:28 "**And the scripture was fulfilled, which saith, And he was numbered with the transgressors.**"

25. Mark 16:9-16 *omitted or put in brackets/footnotes. Contains a powerful Continuationism verse as well as the biblical command to preach the gospel to everyone. For the sake of space I won't list all the verses here.*

26. Luke 4:4 "**but by every word of God**"

A phrase that stresses the importance of God's word, sure it's in Matthew 4:4 but that doesn't make it ok to omit it here.

27. Luke 8:43 "**which had spent all her living upon physicians,**"

28. Luk 9:56 "**For the Son of man is not come to destroy men's lives, but to save *them.***"

This would refute the Catholic inquisition that occurred hundreds of years ago.

29. *Luk 11:4* "**but deliver us from evil**"

30. Luke 17:36 "**Two men shall be in the field; the one shall be taken, and the other left.**"

31. Luke 23:17 "(**For of necessity he must release one unto them at the feast.)**"

32. Luk 23:34 "**Then said Jesus, Father, forgive them; for they know not what they do.**"

Some translations bracket these words saying some manuscripts doesn't have these words, casting doubt on it's authenticity. This passage has Jesus loving his enemies even why he was dying on that cross, I hate to use an emotional appeal but I can't see how this wasn't in the original. It is so like Jesus for him to say something like this.

33. Luke 23:42 "**Lord**" (NLT)

Romans 10:13.

34. John 1:27 "**is preferred before me,**"

35. John 3:13 omits "**which is in heaven**" (NIV)

A powerful phrase showing Jesus omnipresence even on earth.

36. John 3:16 "**begotten**"

Adam was a son of God, Christians are sons of God, angels are sons of God, this omission makes the bible have a contradiction (See Luk 3:38, Job 1&2, John 1:12).

37. John 5:4 "**For an angel went down at a certain season into the pool, and troubled the water: whosoever then first after the troubling of the water stepped in was made whole of whatsoever disease he had.**"

38. John 6:47 "**on me**"

This is an important phrase to Leave out (John 14:6, Acts 4:12). It is only through Jesus that we are saved, not Buddha, nor Muhammad, nor Joseph Smith.

39. John 7:8 "**yet**" (NLT)

Jesus lied?

40. John 8:1-11 *For the sake of space I won't list all these verses here. This is the account of the woman caught in adultery where Jesus forgives her and tells her to sin no more.*

41. Acts 1:3 omits "**infallible**" (DARBY)

42. Acts 8:37 "**And Philip said, If thou believest with all thine heart, thou mayest. And he answered and said, I believe that Jesus Christ is the Son of God.**"

Despite what some may say, this omission does affect doctrine (believer's baptism). You must believe in order to be water baptized. This is a proof text against infant baptism.

43. Acts 15:34 "**Notwithstanding it pleased Silas to abide there still.**"

44. Acts 24:7 "**But the chief captain Lysias came upon us, and with great violence took him away out of our hands,**"

45. Acts 28:29 "**And when he had said these words, the Jews departed, and had great reasoning among themselves.**"

46. Romans 8:1 "**who walk not after the flesh, but after the Spirit.**"

Shows those who are in Christ.

47. Romans 10:7 omits "**again**" (NKJV)

Attacks the resurrection of Jesus.

48. Rom 13:9 "**Thou shalt not bear false witness,**" (NIV)

49. Rom 13:13 "**chambering**"

Omits one of if not the only command not to co-habitate.

50. Romans 16:24 "**The grace of our Lord Jesus Christ be with you all. Amen.**"

51. 1 Corinthians 6:9 removes "**effeminate**"

Although offensive to some, this word points out that certain characteristics in men are not fit for heaven, it's either talking about soft men, or feminized men.

52. 1 Cor 6:20 "**and in your spirit, which are God's.**"

This phrase shows who owns you.

53. 1 Cor 7:5 omits "**fasting and**"

One of the few places in the New Testament that mentions fasting. Additionally in the context of while abstaining from martial relations.

54. 1 Cor 11:29 "**unworthily**"

This omission makes taking the Lord's supper always dangerous.

55. Eph 3:9 removed "**by Jesus Christ:**"

Omits the fact that God used Jesus to create everything.

56. Ephesians 5:30 "**of his flesh, and of his bones**"

57. Colossians 1:14 omits "**through his blood,**" (NIV)

See Leviticus 17:11 and Hebrews 9:22.

58. 1 Tim 6:5 **"from such withdraw thyself"** (ASV)

Removes a biblical command.

59. Titus 2:4 "**sober**" omitted (NASB95)

60. Hebrews 7:21 removes "...**after the order of Melchisedec:**)"(NIV)

61. James 5:16 "**effectual fervent**" missing (RSV)

So what kind of prayer avails much then?

62. 1 Peter 2:2 OMITS "**of the word**" (NLT)

I can see why this translation would diminish the importance of God's word in this verse, shame. Unless I'm mistaken the New Living Translation is a dynamic equivalent translation which is a thought for thought translation, either that or a paraphrase.

63. 1 Peter 4:14 "**on their part he is evil spoken of, but on your part he is glorified. **"

64. 2 Pet 1:21 omits "**holy**" (RSV)

65. 1 John 5:7 "**the Father, the Word, and the Holy Ghost: and these three are one.**"

This is an important verse on the doctrine of the trinity that is omitted some translations, does your bible have it?

66. Jude 1:12 removed "**twice**" (CEV)

67. Revelation 1:11 "**I am Alpha and Omega, the first and the last:**"(NIV)

A powerful verse supporting the deity of Christ Jesus, removed.

68. Rev 11:17 OMITS **"and art to come"** (ESV)

Now why would a verse supporting the future of God's existence not be in the bible?

69. Rev 20:9 omits **"from God"**(NIV)

So who sent the fire?

70. Rev 21:24 **"of them which are saved"** (NLT, NIV)

Removing this may allow for the false teaching of universalism.

Chapter 9: Worst Corruption Awards, 280+ Changes You Should Know

For this last chapter in my book I will be giving my _thoughts, opinions, remarks, and/or comments_ on various readings on over 20 different bible translations or paraphrases (when compared to the KJV). I will **NOT** be including the actual verses themselves so that I will not have to worry about copyright infringement. However I encourage the reader to grab their phone with their favorite bible app and follow along (there are plenty of bible apps and websites that will give you the different translation of most of these verses for free). My suggestions include Blue Letter Bible, You Version, Bible Gateway and Bible Study Tools.

The translations mentioned in this chapter include the New International Version (NIV), New American Standard Version (NASB), New King James (NKJV), The Living Bible (TLB), New Living Translation (NLT), Young's Literal Translation (YLT), Revised Standard Version (RSV), New Revised Standard Version (NRSV), Contemporary English Version (CEV), English Standard Version (ESV), New Century Version (NCV), New World Translation (NWT), The Clear Word (TCW), The Message, The Word on the Street, Good As New Bible (GAN), Good News for Modern Man, God's Word Translation (GWT), The Passion Translation (TPT), The Mirror Bible, The Bible in Basic English (BBE), Darby, The Queen James (QJV), Lexham English Bible (LEB), and the NET Bible (NET).

1. Genesis 1:2 (NWT) An attack on the person-hood of the Spirit.
2. Gen 1: 5 (RSV) The rendering of this verse for this translation makes room for the GAP theory, it is important to have The first day so as not to give evolution a foot in the door so to speak.
3. Gen 1:8 (RSV) See last point.
4. Gen 3:17-19 (MSG) I'm not sure it is accurate to compare men's labor to childbirth.
5. Gen 9:3 (TCW) This rendering may give room for the false teaching that the dietary laws of Leviticus 11 are still binding today.

6. Gen 10:8 (RSV) Doesn't this contradict Gen 6:4.
7. Gen 12:19 (Darby) This verse can be implied to mean that Pharaoh slept with Sarah.
8. Gen 18:5 (BBE) A possible attack on God's omnipotence.
9. Gen 19:5 (QJV) This passage has been changed in order to not condemn consensual gay S*X for the LGBTQ Agenda.
10. Gen 19 (Word on the Street) The contention I have with this paraphrase is that it infers that there were three angels that entered Sodom, but the Lord ain't no angel.
11. Gen 21:6-7 (Word on the Street) This paraphrase is inaccurate, Sarah was 90 when she bore Isaac, thus she would've given suck in her 90's.
12. Gen 21:9 (RSV), The RSV is way less accurate than the KJV in how Ishmael treated Isaac, see Galatians 4:29.
13. Gen 22:8 (NKJV) Changed proof text of Jesus' divinity (John 1:29).
14. Gen 22:18 (NLT) Contradicts Galatians 3:16.
15. Gen 32:32 (NKJV) Different part of the anatomy.
16. Gen 37:3-4 (MSG) This rendering tells us that Joseph's brothers wouldn't say anything to him, KJV tells us they wouldn't "speak peaceably" with Joseph. This means they could have insulted and teased him.
17. Exodus 1:16 (LEB) The rendering of this translation speaks of the male anatomy.
18. Exodus 4:25 (CEV) This translation/paraphrase seems to have Moses' wife calling him her son. Kind of confusing.
19. Exodus 5:5 (TCW) Adventist are trying to make the sabbath rule transcend the Mosaic law, just like the meats.
20. Exodus 31:13-16 (TCW) The Clear Word translation removes the fact that mandatory sabbath keeping was for Israel, not gentiles.
21. Leviticus 15:2 (CEV) Way too graphic, speaks of male anatomy that has an infection.
22. Lev 16:10 Some translations have them send the goat to a demon. This seems questionable.
23. Leviticus 18:22Adds (QJV) The rendering of the passage in this bible makes homosexuality only a sin when done in a pagan temple.
24. Lev 18:23 (NLT) Does not prohibit same sex bestiality for women.

25. Leviticus 20:13 (QJV) Similar to #25.
26. Num 5:27 (NIV) The NIV translation seems to imply inducing an abortion.
27. Num 11:15 (GNT) Attack on Moses' character.
28. Num 16:32 (ESV) Contradicts Numbers 26:11, his children lived.
29. Num 30:6 (TLB) This translation completely messes up the timing of when she may have made a vow (prior to marriage).
30. Deuteronomy 5:3 (TCW) This "Translation" has the complete opposite meaning of the KJV and is inaccurate. God didn't make the Mosaic covenant with Israel until after the Exodus from Egypt.
31. Deut 5:11 (TLB) removes admonition to not use God's name flippantly, only prohibits it when making false vows.
32. Deut 7:7 (DARBY) Different rendering from KJV, was the children of Israel the fewest of all people at that moment?
33. Deut 17:18-20 (MSG) There is a passage in this paraphrase about ordering the king not to make his on version of the bible, is this some sort of jab at the KJV?
34. Deut 18:10 (GW) Doesn't prohibit all magic, just the black kind.
35. Deut 22:28 (NIV) A common argument against the bible is the claim that God condones rape by saying a woman must marry her rapist. While this is the rendering of this version, the KJV for instance doesn't necessarily mean that. I believe the KJV is referring to seduction of a woman.
36. Deut 32:22 (NLT) No hell?
37. Joshua 2:21 (MSTC) The cord represents Jesus blood, so it can't be the color stated here.
38. Judges 4:21 (MSG) I'm not sure how many translations have Sisera thrashing about like this, but I doubt very many.
39. Judges 5:30 (ESV) A woman is more than just her body.
40. Judges 15:16 (YLT) A rather vulgar way to render this passage, isn't it derogatory to use that word when referring to the behind?
41. Judges 15:14-16 (MSG) Doesn't say how many people Samson killed.
42. Judg 16:28 (RSV) It was for both of his eyes.
43. Ruth 1:17 (MSG) The rendering of this verse in the Message is telling us that Ruth believes basically nothing will separate her from Naomi.

44. Ruth 2:7 (RSV) So Ruth didn't rest at all? KJV states otherwise.
45. Ruth 2:7 (TLB) This paraphrase doesn't give exactly where Ruth rested.
46. 1 Samuel 1 :24 (NLT) Confuses quantity with age.
47. 1 Samuel13:1 (ESV) This passage seems to imply that Saul was a baby when he became king.
48. 1 Sam 15:22-23 (MSG) While the KJV has rebellion = witchcraft, this paraphrase has rebellion > witchcraft.
49. 1 Sam 21:6 (RSV) The way that the RSV puts this makes it seem like they are supporting the doctrine of transubstantiation.
50. 2 Samuel 5:21 (NIV) Did Catholics make this to support adopting idols?
51. 2 Samuel 21:19 (ESV) Who killed Goliath?, see 1 Chro 20:5.
52. 2 Sam 22:6 (NLT) Omits hell.
53. 2 Samuel 23:5 (RSV) Is David's house so with God or not?
54. 2 Samuel 24:13 (NLT) Too lazy to address a supposed contradiction?
55. 1 King 14:24 (NIV) Removes sodomite and/or sodomites.
56. 1King 15:12 (NLT) See last point.
57. 1 King 16:33 (CEV) I'm going to be honest here, I just prefer the King James word "grove" in this and other passages because passages that condemn groves are good ammunition against the celebration of Christmas.
58. 1 King 22:38 (NIV) I like to know where they came up with the idea of washing harlots in this passage.
59. 2 King 21:1-6 (MSG) Though this passage may be true, there is do difference between different kinds of magic.
60. 2 King 23:29 (NKJV) Did Pharaohnechoh help the king of Assyria or not?
61. 1 Chro 10:1-22:16 The way this "bible" phrases it leads to the conclusion that David was trusting in his flesh or his own forces rather that God. Is this what the text actually says according to other versions, I doubt it.
    (Street).
62. 2 Chronicles 22:2 (NLT) Too lazy to address supposed contradiction? Age of Ahaziah.

63. Ezra 2:62 (YLT) Wording makes it look like being a priests is bad.

64. Ezra 3:11-13 (MSG) While the KJV has men weeping and others shouting for joy, this bible has them weeping joyfully.

65. Ezra 8:5 (NCV)Adds a name that is not is some translations.

66. Ezra 8:10 (NCV) Adds a name that is not in some translations.

67. Nehemiah 2:2 (MSG) Different emotion.

68. Nehemiah 2:13 (NIV) Omits dragons (maybe for evolution agenda).

69. Nehemiah 5:5 (CEV) How is being brought into bondage the same as being sexually forced?

70. Job 2:9 (YLT) What did Job's wife actually say for Job to do?

71. Job 4:17 (RSV) This translation gives a rhetorical question asking if a man can be upright and/or innocent before his creator (again, I'm only using similar wording to avoid copyright infringement). The answer is actually yes, we are upright before God due to the substitution death of Jesus on the cross for our sins. The question should say can a man be more just or pure than his maker? Which is of coarse not.

72. Job 6:6 (ESV) I list this verse here because I know some people complain about archaic words in the KJV, unless your a genius I doubt you know to what this passage is referring to.

73. Job 3:17 (CEV) Contradicts Isaiah 57:20.

74. Job 10:1-3, 8 (Street) Has Job accusing God of a most deplorable act.

75. Job 21:13 (RSV) Contradicts Isaiah 48:22, 57:21.

76. Job 31:1 (NKJV) Even if this translation is accurate to the verse, I prefer the KJV due to the discouragement of thought crimes.

77. Job 40:15 (TLB) This passage is supposed to refer to a sauropod dinosaur, but this paraphrase changes the animal, is it because of the Evolution agenda?

78. Job 41:1 (TLB) I'm skeptical of the type of animal that this paraphrase is referring to.

79. Psalms 2:12 (RSV) Omits the word Son, an obvious reference to Christ.

80. Psalm 8:5 (NASB95) A little lower than who?

81. Psa 9:17 (NLT) What about Hell?

82. Psa 10:4-5 (NIV) The NIV in this passage is basically telling us that

evil men get wealthy, when it should say that there ways are grievous.

83. Psalms 12:7 (NASB95) An attack on the preservation doctrine.

84. Psa 34:20 (GNT) Destroys messianic prophecy.

85. Psalms 66:18 (BBE) Removes the part about If he regards iniquity.

86. Psa 78:36 (YLT) Attack on God's omniscience, you can't trick God.

87. Psa 100:5 (RSV) Another attack on preservation doctrine.

88. Psa 116:3 (NIV) Hell omitted.

89. Psa 138:2 (RSV) While this translation puts the word and God's name on equal footing, the KJV exalts the word higher.

90. Psa 148:7 (NKJV) I mention this because I believe It's important to keep dragons in the bible because it's evidence of dinosaurs with man, and thus a young earth.

91. Proverbs 3:21-26 (MSG) A false promise that certain things listed in this passage will upkeep your appearance.

92. Prov 5:5 (NLT) Omits hell.

93. Pro 6:30 (RSV) The RSV has the opposite meaning of the KJV, are thieves despised when they steal to keep from starving.

94. Pro 7:27 (NIV) Omits hell.

95. Prov 10:27 "...adds hours to each day;..." (TLB) A false statement, a virtuous person may end up living the full amount they were intended to but there are still only 24 hrs per day.

96. Proverbs 11:16 (NKJV) Encouraging wickedness? Be bad to keep wealth?

97. Pro 11:30 (NIV) Loses evangelism component.

98. Prov 12:4 (GNT) Endorses pride.

99. Prov 13:6 (LEB) This passage makes no sense with this translation, it is the sinner that is overthrown.

100. Prov 14:1 (MSG) Gender swap.

101. Prov 15:16 (Street) This translation seems to imply debt is OK.

102. Prov 15:33 (TPT). Research the 8 letter S-word here. This is said to be a pagan goddess but is also claimed to be the Holy Spirit. Both cannot be true.

103. Prov 17:6 (NLT) Pride is stated in a positive sense.

104. Prov 17:8 (RSV) This translation seems to be implying that bribery and sorcery is OK.

105. Prov 18:8 (NKJV) Glamorizes gossip.
106. Prov 23:14 (NIV) A bad rendering, we all die, it is hell that you'd be saving your child from by discipline.
107. Prov 23:25 (GNT) Endorsing pride.
108. Prov 23:33 (TLB) This translation list a certain medical condition that one of my former neighbours claimed to have, he would use it as an excuse to drink.
109. Prov 25:23 (NKJV) Compare to KJV, is it coming or going?
110. Pro 27:6 (YLT) This version confuses quantity with falsehood.
111. Pro 29:21 (BBE) This passage seemingly implies your should mistreat your servants/slaves.
112. Prov 30:28 (NLT) In my opinion this passage is supposed to be claiming that we should look to the spider as an example of the reward of hard work, loses meaning in this translation, or paraphrase I should say.
113. Ecclesiastes 1:1 (MSG) While the title given to King Solomon here is unique, is it accurate?
114. Ecclesiastes 2:8 (MSG) Although Solomon may have been referring to women to sleep with in this verse, the symbolism to musical instruments I find to be of more better quality than Mr. Peterson's rendition. So this may not have been a corruption as much as just a preference on my behalf.
115. Ecclesiastes 3:12 (NLT) Embracing hedonism!!!
116. Ecclesiastes 7:26-29 (MSG) Not true. Solomon said he didn't find one woman among a thousand, he did find one man among a thousand.
117. Ecclesiastes 8:10 (NLT) How were the wicked treated?
118. Ecc 9:15 (GNT) Did he save the town or not?
119. Ecclesiastes 11:10 (RSV) Instead of an admonition against sinning the RSV is telling us to avoid pain. I could see this verse being used to endorse pharmakeia.
120. Ecclesiastes 12:1 (YLT) Endorsing polytheism.
121. Song of Solomon 1:4 "...rightly do they love you." (NKJV) If this passage has a spiritual connotation of Christ Jesus and the church then it could be stating a characteristic of the upright (to love Jesus),

this would be missing in this translation.

122. Song of Solomon 1:12 (CEV) Magic being used in a positive sense, even if it was figuratively speaking.

123. Song of Solomon 2:13 (TPT) **Adds nearly 50 words**

124. Song of Solomon 2:3-4 (MSG) I personally, am the Christian that believes that even reading romance novels are wrong, so I also think that Eugene Peterson's the Message less than subtle and not so poetic renderings *(in some places)* of the Song of Solomon can be inappropriate for some younger audiences (to say the least), I much prefer the symbolic imagery of the KJV myself.

125. Song of Solomon 4:6-7 (MSG) See last point.

126. Song of Solomon 7:1-2 (GNT) See point 124 also.

127. Isa 3:2 (NLT) The passage of this translation seems to imply that they needed a certain type of diviner.

128. Isa 4:1 (MSG) This is passage may be referring to Christ and the church, so I am not sure about how the message worded this one.

129. Isa 7:14 (RSV) An Attack on the virgin birth.

130. Isa 7:20 (NIV) Is the NIV referring to the genitals here?

131. Isa 9:3 (NKJV) Was the joy increased or not?

132. Isa 14:12 (CEV) Gives Satan Jesus title (Revelation 22:16).

133. Isa 14:15 (NCV) Doesn't condemn Satan to hell.

134. Isa 19:18 (MSG) The Message gives a very interesting title to the city in this paraphrase bible. Eugene doesn't call it the city of destruction like the KJV, instead he calls it something else. We know sun worship is contemned in many places in scripture (Deut 4:19, 2 King 23:5, Jer 8:2).

135. Isa 66:5 (NKJV) Omits "...but he shall appear to..." If this verse is referring to the rapture or second coming then omitting this phrase eliminates this proof text.

136. Jeremiah 3:23 (ESV) Kinda sexually graphic.

137. Jer 5:17 (NLT) This may be the only translation that I have found that is referring to cannibalism in this passage.

138. Jeremiah 8:8 (RSV) Another attack on the doctrine of preservation?

139. Jeremiah 9:26 (GWT) This translation gives the opposite meaning of the KJV. The KJV says that the nations are uncircumcised.

140. Ezekiel 2:6 (RSV) Not sure about the accuracy of this one, what is it about Ezekiel and scorpions?
141. Ezekiel 10:14 (NLT) What about the cherub?
142. Ezekiel 16:49 (NCV) Comfort isn't in itself evil, See 2 Corinthians 1:3-4.
143. Daniel 7:5 (NRSV) This version changes ribs to the bones that are on either side of an elephant's trunk.
144. Daniel 7:13 (NCV) This version removes the title of Jesus (Son of man).
145. Daniel 9:26 (RSV) In addition to eliminating the meaning of substitution atonement, this version also claims that Jesus loses it all.
146. Daniel 12:1 (BBE) This version destroys a possible pre-tribulation rapture verse.
147. Hosea 11:12 (NIV) This version says the opposite of the KJV, NLT, ASV, and NKJV. It's saying Judah is against God in this passage.
148. Hosea 13:9 (RSV) Who destroyed Israel?
149. Hosea 13:14 (CEV) This passage of the CEV contradicts the KJV, see 1 Cor 15:54-55 to find out the true reading.
150. Amos 4:4 (ESV) Was this a verse change in order to make people tithe more often?
151. Amos 7:14 (RSV) If Amos is claiming not to be a prophet, then how can we take his words as authoritative?
152. Jonah 4:7 (NCV) This version seems to think that plants are alive in the biblical sense, plants do not die, they wither.
153. Nahum 1:3 (TLB) An attack on God's Character! Contradicts Psalms 86:5.
154. Nahum 1:8 (RSV) Who is pursuing the enemies?
155. Nahum 1:9 (YLT) Is Nahum plotting against the Lord too?
156. Nahum 2:2 (MSG) Is God endorsing pride in this paraphrase?
157. Nahum 3:4 (YLT) The way that this translation describes this mistress, it makes it sound positive.
158. Micah 1:8 (NCV) omits dragons.
159. Micah 1:8 (NKJV) omits dragons.
160. Micah 3:5 (MSG) Having the bible using the G.D word is a bit too much for my taste.

161. Micah 5:2 (NIV) An attack on the deity of Christ, by making him not eternal.
162. Zephaniah 2:3 (NLT) Another Pre-trib rapture verse obliterated!
163. Zeph 3:9 (CEV) Puts the word language in the plural sense here, I believe this is wrong because I think this actually teaches that the Lord will give us all just one language near the end of time, see 1 Corinthians 13:8.
164. Hab 3:5 (NLT) I think this change is significant because I use this verse in KJV to expose Santa.
165. Habbakuk 3:6 (ESV) Contradicts Malachi 3:6, and Hebrews 13:8.
166. Zech 13:6 (MSG) A change in where the Messiah was wounded.
167. Mal 1:3 (NKJV) Omits dragons (Significant for us YEC'S).
168. Mal 2:15 (NIV) Has the wrong meaning, it should be talking about God making husband and wife one flesh.
169. Mal 2:16 (NIV) This verse should be saying how God hates putting away!
170. Mat 3:4 (GAN) Has quite a unique reading of what John ate so I question it's authenticity.
171. Mat 3:16 (GAN) Misgendering the Holy Spirit.
172. Matthew 4:4 (TPT) The way this translation puts it makes one question whether or not the canon is closed.
173. Mat 18:9 (TCW) Supports the false doctrine of Annihilation-ism.
174. Matt 18:22 (CEV) Way less forgiveness.
175. Mat 24:48 (MSG) **Hell is not cold!**
176. Matthew 25:46 (NWT) Another change to support annihilation-ism.
177. Mat 27:19 (NLT) When was her dream?
178. Mat 28:17 (YLT) Diminishes the fact that Jesus was divine by omitting worship.
179. Mark 1:2 (NCV) Should say prophets.
180. Mark 1:41 (NIV) This translation attacks Jesus' character by having him be angry at this leper it's the opposite meaning of the KJV and contradicts the context.
181. Mark 8:36 (RSV) Was this change made to support the false teaching of Annihilation-ism?

182. Luke 2:22 (NLT) Defiles Jesus' sinlessness.

183. Luke 2:43 (ESV) Attacks Jesus as being the son of God.

184. Luke 4:18 (Mirror) Listed because of the strange wording, Is this passage deifying man?

185. Luk 7:43-47 (Street) The way this "bible" phrases these verses makes no sense. Anything poured as an offering on Jesus feet would not be a waste, and Jesus wouldn't say it was.

186. Luke 12:46 (MSG) Diminishing the threat Hell.

187. Luke 16:19-30 (TCW) This "bible" tells us these verses are just a story to promote soul sleep false doctrine.

188. Luk 18:25 (TPT) This is probably the first and only time that I have seen a bible version switch the word needle for something you would use to tie someone up. Definitely not the same thing.

189. Luke 23:32 (NET) Jesus wasn't a rule breaker.

190. Luke 23:43 (TCW) Used to perpetuate soul sleep myth.

191. Luke 23:43 (NWT) Used to perpetuate soul sleep myth.

192. John 1:1 (NWT) An attack on Jesus Deity.

193. John 1:12 (Mirror bible) Jesus is the only begotten Son, we are adopted into the family.

194. John 1:13 (Mirror) See last point, additionally the way this verse is phrased, only a complete Narcissist would believe it.

195. John 1:18 (NASB95) Jesus Divinity wasn't begotten.

196. John 1:42 (TPT) Jesus is the Rock, not Peter. Obviously Catholics think Jesus was referring to Peter when declaring that on this rock he would build his church. See 1 Corinthians 10:4.

197. John 3:7 (Mirror). This version attacks the need to be born again!

198. John 17:7 (Mirror) This passage is quite confusing but seems to deify man.

199. John 20:28 (original clear word) Attacks Jesus' divinity, by taking out the fact that Thomas called Jesus God.

200. Acts 8:20 (GNT) Peter cursing Simon.

201. Acts 17:22 (NIV) Passage should be condemning superstition, not religion.

202. Act 20:7 (TCW) This change by the Adventist bible "the Clear Word) might have been made to support the false teaching that

Christians must observe the Sabbath.

203. Acts 20:28 (RSV) Attacks Jesus' divinity by omitting the fact that we were redeemed by God's blood.

204. Rom 1:26-27 (QJV) This "translation" gives the act of homosexuality a religious connotation in this passage in order to not condemn regular homosexual acts.

205. Rom 1:26-27"God let them go on to pursue their selfish desires. Women use their charms to further their own ends. Men, instead of being friends, ruthlessly exploit one another." (GAN)

206. Rom 12:6 (TPT) I mention this verse from the Passion Translation because I don't know where in the bible Brian Simmon's gets that we have to some how trigger, or turn on our gift.

207. 1 Corinthians 1:12 (TPT) Gives a commentary here instead of translating the text.

208. 1 Corinthians 8:4 (NASB95) It appears this translation doesn't believe idols are real.

209. 1 Cor 9:27 (DARBY) Endorsing Self flagellation.

210. 1 Corinthians 11:4 (TPT) Brian adds his own ideas and thoughts to the text that isn't found in the Greek, this may pass as a commentary in this verse but this verse was not translated correctly.

211. 1 Corinthians 11:5 (TPT) Similar to number 210 but even worse! At least the last passage could have been implying the meaning that Brian inserted, with this there is no hint that it's talking about a woman in a position of a leader here.

212. 1 Corinthians 11:16 (RSV) Opposite meaning of KJV, actually makes short hair on men mandatory.

213. 1 Cor 11:29 (RSV) Everyone will be judged so this rendering is less serious that the KJV'S rendering me thinks.

214. 1 Cor 12:6-7 (TPT) There are two problems that I find with this "Translations" rendering of verses 6 and 7. In verse 6 we again see the talk of turning our gift on or triggering them, is this biblical? Secondly, I can see how some "believers" may use verse seven to teach that the canon of scripture is still open.

215. 1 Cor 13:4 (RSV) Love is Jealous, God is love and he is jealous for his church.

216. 1 Cor 13:5 (NIV) This translation actually says that we should forget how people treated us, yes we should forgive but not forget. We are told to mark and avoid certain people.
217. 2 Cor 1:12 (GNT) Pride is a sin.
218. 2 Cor 2:17 (NIV) Quite pertinent to this issue indeed. The removal of the word corrupt from this passage completely changes the meaning of the verse.
219. 2 Cor 4:14 (NKJV) Presupposes Jesus not risen.
220. 2 Cor 7:14 (NLT) Pride being used in a positive way.
221. 2 Cor 11:21-12:10 (Street) I see two problems with these passages; they double the time that Paul was stranded in the ocean and they presume that Paul didn't die by stoned and was brought back to life. In the KJV it's verse 11:25, Chapter 11.
222. Galatians 5:12 (GNT). This translation has Paul wanting people to neuter themselves.
223. Galatians 5:21 (NASB95) Says it's a sin to be jealous.
224. Gal 5:20 (GNT) Makes ambition a bad thing.
225. Galatians 6:4 (GNT) Endorsing pride.
226. Eph 4:6 (street) Only the born again has the Spirit of Christ.
227. Ephesians 5:8-14 (Word on the Street) actually verse 18 in KJV, irreverently commands us to get inebriated on our maker.
228. Ephesians 5:18 (ESV) .Omits moderation clause
229. Epheshian 5 (TPT) The author of the Passion Translation doesn't seem to like the word submit in the context of husbands and wives. Instead he switches out for another word that doesn't mean the same thing. It is proper for a wife to submit to her husband, for children to their parents and an employee to his boss, it doesn't make one inferior to the other, Christ is fully God and yet Jesus submitted to the Father.
230. Philippians 2:6 (ESV) Attacks Jesus Divinity, by underestimating what Jesus thought about himself. The KJV makes it clear that Jesus knew he was God.
231. Philippians 2:16 (NLT) Justifying Pride.
232. Philippians 3:5 (GNT) Gives a false statement, it is a day short.
233. Philippians 4:13 (NIV) Removes the Name of Christ.
234. Collosians 1:16 (NWT) Inserts a word that isn't in the Greek in

order to Attack Christ divinity.

235. Collosians 2:16-17 (Clear Word for Kids) This verses is phrased in such a way in order to make believers think they have to physically rest on the sabbath to be saved. (Adventists doctrine).

236. Colossians 2:18 (NIV) Did they see it or not?

237. Colossians 3:6 (TPT) This version has God being angry at disobedient behavior, not the person themselves. The truth is that God punishes people for sin, he doesn't punish sin itself.

238. Colossians 3:16 (TPT) Brian Simmons changes spiritual songs (which is the type of songs we should sing) to wording that implies that the Holy Ghost gives us songs to sing prophetically. I personally never witnessed such music but I'm not saying it doesn't exist. Still I'm not sure I agree with this rendering.

239. Colossions 3:20 (TPT) I ask the reader to check this "Translation" and tell me if this reading means obedience.

240. Colossians 4:15 (NLT) Different gender.

241. 1 Thess 2:7 (LEB) Illogical, how are babies synonymous with breastfeeding moms?

242. 1 Thess 2:20 (GNT) Another passage with pride in the positive sense.

243. 1 Thess 5:22 (NKJV) Don't do it if it even looks wrong, is what is should mean.

244. 2 Thess 1:9 (TLB) Hell is caste into the lake of fire, therefore it cannot be permenant.

245. 2 Thess 2:3 (GNT) I believe the Good News Translation has an incorrect view of Eschatology here. Without quoting it, it seems to say that the day of Christ will not come until the last insurrection occurs, that isn't necessarily true. Since there is at least a thousand year gap between when the man of sin is revealed and cast into the lake of fire to when Satan is loosed from the pit to gather Gog and Magog (which is the last insurrection in my estimation, see Revelation 20). During that 1000 year interval Christ sets up the Millennial kingdom.

246. 2 Thess 3:11 (YLT) I have included this book, chapter, and verse of the Young's Literal Translation because to me, this passage makes no

sense, this translations seems to be telling us that some people are not working, and at the same time working too much. This seems contradictory.

247. 1 Timothy 2:11 (TPT) This translation adds extra criteria that you won't find in the Greek. That they are recently turned Christians. This passage is supposed to be referring to wives.

248. 1 Tim 2:15 (CEV) This translation appears to be teaching works-based salvation.

249. 1 Tim 3:2 (NIV) Doesn't forbid polygamy.

250. 1 Timothy 3:16 (NIV) Who appeared in the flesh?

251. 1 Tim 4:3 (TCW) This verse is phrased in a way to put Christians under the Leviticus food laws.

252. 1 Tim 5:16 (NLT) Shifts all responsibility to the women.

253. 1 Tim 6:5 (ESV) It is really easy to interpret this passage in this version to support the prosperity gospel.

254. 1 Timothy 6:20 (NIV) It's literally the worst time in history to remove the word science here, even if they mean the same thing, or come from the same Greek word. (Evolution Agenda)?

255. 2 Tim 2:16 (TLB) It's not a sin to be angry at someone with good reason, see Eph 4:26.

256. 2 Tim 2:15 (RSV) Omits the command to study.

257. 2 Tim 3:5 (NLT) Godliness doesn't necessarily equal religiosity, there are many ungodly religions in the world.

258. Titus 1:6 (NIV) Like 1 Timothy 3 also removes the monogamy requirement.

259. Titus 3:10 (NKJV) Christians are supposed to be divisive in some situations, see Mat 10:34-35. It's heretics we are supposed to reject.

260. Hebrews 1:8 (NWT) Omits God calling Jesus God.

261. Hebrews 2:16 (NIV) This version isn't talking about the incarnation is this verse.

262. Hebrews 3:16 (NKJV) Factually inaccurate, what about Joshua and Caleb?

263. Hebrews 11:1-3 (Word on the Street) Faith is not the absence of evidence, while it is true we walk by faith and not sight (2Cor 5:7), there are plenty of reasons to believe that Christ is who he says he is,

his miracles prove his words. See John 10:38, 14:11, 20:30-31.

264. James 1:9 (NIV) Supporting the notion that one should be proud.

265. James 1:26 (TLB) Vain means futile and/or worthless. It doesn't imply that this man's religion has some value.

266. James 3:12 (NASB20) Contains a scientific error, we can get fresh water from the oceans by the hydro-logic cycle.

267. James 4:5 (NASB20) God isn't Created.

268. 1 Peter 1:22-25 (street) The meaning for the endurance of the word of God was shifted from for ever to not necessarily that.

269. 1 Peter 3:1 (RSV) This version is kinda telling women to shut it. The passage should be referring to the word aka the bible.

270. 1 Peter 3:19-22 (MSG) Water baptism saves not!

271. 1 Peter 5:2 (GNT) This translation gives the part about money a less negative connotation.

272. 1 John 1:8 (NET) This version implies that believers still are guilty of sin.

273. 1 John 2:17 (YLT) This translation really seems to hack off our gift of eternal life.

274. 3:18 (YLT) This translation seems to omit the action part of Love. Galatians 6:10, James 2:16.

275. 1 John 5:19 (NLT) This translation gives Satan way too much power. The world is wicked though.

276. 1 John 5:21 (street) I just find this passage to be irreverent, the bible says be sober 1 Peter 5:8.

277. 2 John 1:7 (NIV) Is this supposed to be past, present or future tense? Different translations, different tenses.

278. 2 Jon 1:10 (NKJV) Bidding Godspeed isn't the same at saying hello.

279. Jude 1:7 (QJV) Obviously they worded this to allow for homosexuality.

280. Jude 1:9 (TCW) This verse was changed by Adventist to support the false teaching that Jesus is the famous archangel who's name starts with M.

281. Jude 1:19 (GW) Omits the reference to the Holy Spirit.

282. Jude 1:19 (NWT) Another change the JW's made in order to cancel the personhood of the Spirit.

283. Rev 8:13 (NIV) Are we talking about an angel here or some type of winged fowl?

284. Rev 11:9 (TLB) You won't get a prophecy that requires television or internet with this change.

285. Rev 11:17-18 (street) This paraphrase seems to have a Pagan goddess helping the woman (It's ACTUALLY verse 12:16 in the KJV).

286. Rev 13:1 (NIV) Who stood on the shore?

287. Rev 15:5-8 (MSG) Being able and allowed are to different things.

Finished.

Don't miss out!

Visit the website below and you can sign up to receive emails whenever Justin Horn publishes a new book. There's no charge and no obligation.

https://books2read.com/r/B-A-KAVIB-LHUQD

BOOKS 2 READ

Connecting independent readers to independent writers.

Also by Justin Horn

The Apologetic Series
An Overwhelming Case For The Christian Worldview
Addressing Alleged Bible Contradictions And Exposing Bible Corruptions
The Greatest Gamble

The Bible Study Series
Bible Verses For Born-Again Believers
Bible Verses For Born Again Believers Volume 2: Sin, The Devil, & Hell
Bible Verses For Born-Again Believers Vol. 3

Standalone
Schooling and Gender Roles From The Christian Perspective